# seeing**red** 2012

Published in 2012 by
The Original Double Red Ltd
4 Gateway Court
Dankerwood Road
South Hykeham
Lincoln LN6 9UL

Tel: +44 (0)1522 693 278
www.doublered.co.uk

ISBN 978-0-9534420-9-6

Photography and Copyright of all images
Double Red

Photographers
James Wright
Keith Lock
Sue Ward
Dave Yeomans
Pete Denton
David Reygondeau
Bonnie Lane (Ducati 848)

Project Manager
Sue Ward

Picture Editors
James Wright
Sue Ward
Katie Ward

Contributors
Dave Fern
Sue Jobling
Phil Wain

Contributing Editor
Larry Carter

Design and Layout
Kubed Design

Results and Statistics
Timing Solutions Ltd. www.tsl-timing.com

Special Thanks to:
The organisers and sponsors involved in the MCE Insurance British Superbike Championship, especially the team at MSVR whose dedication and commitment makes the MCE Insurance British Superbike Championship the strongest domestic championship in the world. Every single person involved in the organisation and running of the championship whose often difficult jobs go unnoticed and unrewarded, they know who they are, the medics, physios, marshals, press officers, scrutineers, journalists, television crews, truck drivers, mechanics, chefs, cleaners, hospitality crews, commentators etc., and last but not least the riders and teams, who seldom complain at 'just one more shot' and make the MCE Insurance British Superbike Championship the amazing spectacle it is.

# Contents

"Four wheels move the body... two wheels move the soul"

- anon

# seeing**red** 2012

The 17th edition of the MCE Insurance British Superbike Championship will go down in history as one of the most significant.

Not for the first time we introduced pioneering new technical regulations which drew attention and praise from around the world. All BSB teams would run a series specified MoTeC ECU and machines would run without rider aids such as traction control. This was done alongside more restrictive engine tuning all to reduce the costs of participation and to enhance both the competitiveness and spectacle. If there was ever any doubt that this was the right move, these changes were unquestionably a significant factor in delivering eight different race winners and a top six classification at the end of the season which consisted off six different teams representing five different manufacturers.

We also had a historic first visit to mainland Europe with a trip across the North Sea to the TT Circuit Assen. The Cathedral of Speed as it's known served up some of the best racing ever seen in BSB. The atmosphere was electric as the dramatic first round of the Showdown kicked off, and at that point the championship was turned well and truly on its head when defending champion Tommy Hill was denied a race start following an incident on route to the starting grid.

As we know ultimately it was Shane 'Shakey' Byrne who was to be crowned champion for a record-equalling third time to match the previous success of just two BSB legends Niall Mackenzie and Ryuichi Kiyonari. Shakey now has just two race wins separating him from equalling Kiyo's record of BSB race victories. However this season has also shown some of the Championship's new contenders in the shape of Alex Lowes, who scored his first wins and Tommy Bridewell who gave BMW their best results in the Championship with fourth places.

This season once again saw a ferocious battle for Motorpoint British Supersport honours, every one of the 24 races a hard-fought contest which produced seven different winners. Podiums throughout the year were separated by fractions of a second, but the final thriller was saved for the last race at Brands Hatch. What should have been a head to head on the race track, was instead an agonising twist that any Hollywood blockbuster movie director would have been proud of.

As always I would like to extend our thanks to all our Championship partners, teams and riders and to my organising colleagues. It is great to know that MCE Insurance will remain title partners of the series until 2018 completing the longest championship title sponsor association in motorcycle racing history. Finally, thank you to the media who write and capture the drama and passion of the season and of course to the BSB fans who are so enthusiastic and devoted to watching every round in all weathers.

I hope you enjoy the remarkable imagery of Double Red as a great record of yet another incredible year.

Stuart Higgs
Series Director
*MCE Insurance British Superbike Championship*

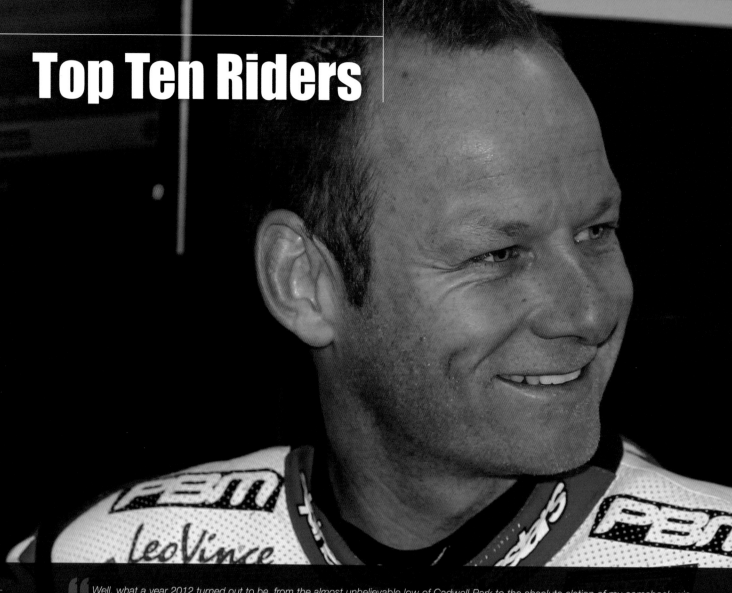

> *Well, what a year 2012 turned out to be, from the almost unbelievable low of Cadwell Park to the absolute elation of my comeback win three and a half weeks after an operation on my shoulder, it's been a long season but a short and intense showdown, fortunately it all worked out cool in the end, that's three titles in the bag now but it only took until the back straight on the cool down lap at Brands to realise that now all I've done is matched two others, I don't want to match people, I want to beat them, all . . . there's quite a few people to thank and probably not enough pages in this book to mention how grateful I am to them, but they know who they are and what part they played and to everyone else who cheered or assisted and supported in any way shape or form, thank you all so very much . . .*

*Shakey #67*
*MCE British Superbike champion 2012*

## Shane Byrne
## Rapid Solicitors Kawasaki

When you consider Shakey took until the sixth race of his campaign to record his first victory, set only one pole position all season and missed four races, it's quite remarkable that he ended up as British Champion for a third time by a healthy 28 points. But Byrne did what he does best and was fast and consistent when it mattered, namely in the Showdown, which hadn't been kind to him the year previous and anyone who scored four wins and three third places would have taken the title in the seven races that matter.

Reunited with the PBM team he'd enjoyed so much success with in the past, the Londoner sustained a nasty shoulder injury which kept him out of Cadwell and Donington but after that inauspicious start, he was soon into his stride and barring a mechanical issue at Snetterton, he finished all of the following races he contested on the podium.

Going into the final race at Brands Hatch, he was champion-elect and didn't have to win, but he did, because he could, and that was the measure of a man who, if he stays in BSB next year, is set to become the most successful BSB rider of all time.

| Results | | | |
|---|---|---|---|
| Position: | 1st | | |
| Points: | 683 | | |
| Qualifying Poles: | 1 | | |
| Fastest Lap Poles: | 0 | | |
| Front Rows: | 11 | | |
| Best Grid: | Pole | | |
| Races: | 22 | | |
| Wins: | 8 | | |
| Podiums: | 10 | | |
| Best Result: | 1st | | |
| Fastest Laps: | 2 | | |
| | | | |
| Brands Hatch Indy: | 7th | | |
| Thruxton: | 4th | 3rd | |
| Oulton Park: | 11th | 2nd | 1st |
| Snetterton: | R | 2nd | |
| Knockhill: | 1st | 2nd | |
| Oulton Park: | 3rd | 3rd | 2nd |
| Brands Hatch GP: | 1st | 1st | |
| Cadwell Park: | Inj | Inj | |
| Donington Park: | Inj | Inj | |
| TT Circuit Assen: | 1st | 2nd | |
| Silverstone: | 2nd | 2nd | |
| Brands Hatch GP: | 1st | 1st | 1st |

# Josh Brookes
## Tyco Suzuki

In most other years, Josh Brookes would have been champion when you consider the fact that the amiable Aussie finished every race and only six times in the entire season was he off the podium. In his second season with the Northern Irish TAS team, only this time without another major Suzuki team in the series, Brookes was a capable challenger but his problem was, he didn't win enough races. He was fast, very fast at times, and his career-first Donington double set things up nicely for the Showdown whereby he left Assen with honours even alongside Byrne with a win and second place each. But from thereon in, Brookes didn't have an answer to the Kawasaki man and had to play second best to his rival in the remaining five races although to his credit, the fact that Josh took it to the final race of the season is testament to his never-say-die attitude. Brookes will be back again in 2013 and already, he is the hot tip to land that elusive first BSB crown.

| Results | | | |
|---|---|---|---|
| Position: | | | 2nd |
| Points: | | | 655 |
| Qualifying Poles: | | | 3 |
| Fastest Lap Poles: | | | 4 |
| Front Rows: | | | 8 |
| Best Grid: | | | Pole |
| Races: | | | 26 |
| Wins: | | | 4 |
| Podiums: | | | 16 |
| Best Result: | | | 1st |
| Fastest Laps: | | | 8 |
| | | | |
| Brands Hatch Indy: | 10th | | |
| Thruxton: | 3rd | 1st | |
| Oulton Park: | 3rd | 3rd | 4th |
| Snetterton: | 3rd | 3rd | |
| Knockhill: | 4th | 4th | |
| Oulton Park: | 2nd | 2nd | 3rd |
| Brands Hatch GP: | 2nd | 2nd | |
| Cadwell Park: | 6th | 2nd | |
| Donington Park: | 1st | 1st | |
| TT Circuit Assen: | 2nd | 1st | |
| Silverstone: | 4th | 3rd | |
| Brands Hatch GP: | 3rd | 2nd | 2nd |

# Tommy Hill
## Swan Yamaha

For much of the season, the defending champion looked odds-on to retain the title he won in the most dramatic of fashions the year previous. Despite an opening round disaster which saw him crash out at Brands Hatch and a mechanical failure at Snetterton, all was looking good for Hill as he breezed into the Showdown and held a massive 40-point lead after his Cadwell Park double. The team tried a new engine at Donington as Hill surrendered a few points but then came the Showdown which effectively negated his points advantage. What happened at Assen couldn't have been scripted and a collision on the grid saw him not score in the opening race to put him on the back foot. A combination of grip and confidence issues saw him put in a lacklustre performance at Silverstone to effectively end his title defence and again, it seemed all was not well at the championship finale at Brands Hatch although a couple of podiums did clinch him third in the standings. A scant reward for a season which promised so much and whether rider, and indeed team, will be back for 2013 remains to be seen.

| Results | | | |
|---|---|---|---|
| Position: | | | 3rd |
| Points: | | | 612 |
| Qualifying Poles: | | | 4 |
| Fastest Lap Poles: | | | 3 |
| Front Rows: | | | 10 |
| Best Grid: | | | Pole |
| Races: | | | 26 |
| Wins: | | | 7 |
| Podiums: | | | 11 |
| Best Result: | | | 1st |
| Fastest Laps: | | | 7 |
| | | | |
| Brands Hatch Indy: | C | | |
| Thruxton: | 2nd | 2nd | |
| Oulton Park: | 1st | 4th | 2nd |
| Snetterton: | 1st | C | |
| Knockhill: | 2nd | 3rd | |
| Oulton Park: | 1st | 1st | 1st |
| Brands Hatch GP: | 3rd | 3rd | |
| Cadwell Park: | 1st | 1st | |
| Donington Park: | 2nd | 3rd | |
| TT Circuit Assen: | R | 4th | |
| Silverstone: | 7th | 7th | |
| Brands Hatch GP: | 2nd | 6th | 3rd |

# Alex Lowes
## Team WFR

| Results | | | |
|---|---|---|---|
| Position: | | | 4th |
| Points: | | | 584 |
| Qualifying Poles: | | | 4 |
| Fastest Lap Poles: | | | 4 |
| Front Rows: | | | 2 |
| Best Grid: | | | Pole |
| Races: | | | 26 |
| Wins: | | | 2 |
| Podiums: | | | 3 |
| Best Result: | | | 1st |
| Fastest Laps: | | | 4 |
| | | | |
| Brands Hatch Indy: | 17th | | |
| Thruxton: | 22nd | 8th | |
| Oulton Park: | C | 10th | 10th |
| Snetterton: | 5th | 6th | |
| Knockhill: | 9th | 8th | |
| Oulton Park: | C | 9th | 6th |
| Brands Hatch GP: | 7th | 6th | |
| Cadwell Park: | 2nd | 4th | |
| Donington Park: | 6th | 5th | |
| TT Circuit Assen: | 3rd | 3rd | |
| Silverstone: | 1st | 1st | |
| Brands Hatch GP: | C | R | C |

Talk about coming good just when it mattered, that's exactly what happened for Alex Lowes as he peaked at the right time but sadly in the end, the very realistic chances he had of lifting the BSB crown faded at the final hurdle. The young Lincoln rider arrived in 2012 very much on the back foot after a damaging season where he rode – and crashed – lots of different bikes. Reunited with the Yorkshire-based WFR team he split with when things were going well at the start of 2011, Lowes sensibly played himself in without looking like a title contender. But gradually, he emerged and blasted his way into contention at his local round at Cadwell Park before claiming the last place in the Showdown at Donington. What happened next was simply amazing as a double podium at Assen was followed by a sensational double win at Silverstone to hold third in the standings just 24 points off the leader Byrne going into Brands. Sadly, the dream faded as a couple of crashes and a mechanical DNF saw him not add to his tally but if nothing else, Alex has firmly put himself in the shop window for a 2013 title tilt.

| 1st Finishing Position | R | Retired | NS | Non Starter |
|---|---|---|---|---|
| C Crashed | Inj. | Injured | Dq | Disqualified |

# Michael Laverty
## Samsung Honda

It would be unfair to say that Michael Laverty under-performed, as anyone who has climbed a BSB podium ten times this season including two wins would vouch, but the stark matter of fact is the likeable Ulsterman under-achieved. Changing teams for the third year in succession can't have helped and the move to the factory-backed Honda, complete with all the additional expectation and pressure certainly looked a heavy burden for Laverty to carry in the first part of the season. But eventually, he turned it round and the challenge gradually began and courtesy of those wins and packing the places, the results came. However, it was the Showdown that proved to be Michael's nemesis as try as he might, he was never really happy with the bike as the grip issues that blighted his campaign early on returned with a vengeance to leave him a lowly fifth in the rankings which is not where he, nor more importantly Honda, expected. If he stays with the Louth-based squad next season, he knows he will have to improve.

**Results**

| | | | |
|---|---|---|---|
| Position: | 5th | | |
| Points: | 581 | | |
| Qualifying Poles: | 0 | | |
| Fastest Lap Poles: | 1 | | |
| Front Rows: | 13 | | |
| Best Grid: | Pole | | |
| Races: | 26 | | |
| Wins: | 2 | | |
| Podiums: | 8 | | |
| Best Result: | 1st | | |
| Fastest Laps: | 3 | | |
| | | | |
| Brands Hatch Indy: | C | | |
| Thruxton: | 6th | 13th | |
| Oulton Park: | 6th | 12th | 7th |
| Snetterton: | 2nd | 1st | |
| Knockhill: | 1st | 2nd | |
| Oulton Park: | C | 4th | 5th |
| Brands Hatch GP: | 4th | 4th | |
| Cadwell Park: | 3rd | 3rd | |
| Donington Park: | 3rd | 2nd | |
| TT Circuit Assen: | 7th | 7th | |
| Silverstone: | 3rd | 5th | |
| Brands Hatch GP: | 10th | 3rd | C |

# Tommy Bridewell
## Supersonic BMW

The very fact that Tommy and his inexperienced Italian team got anywhere near the Showdown was nothing short of heroic and very long odds would have been given at the start of the year, especially seeing as though the deal only came about a couple of days before the opening round at Easter. But Bridewell, lambasted in some quarters after 2011 as a cocky crasher, wasn't about to waste the chance and set about a mature and professional campaign from the opening round. Race by race, the results came and by mid season, he was regularly troubling the BSB elite on a bike which had never proved itself in the UK series. By the Showdown, Bridewell was ready to deliver the team's and BMW's first BSB podium and came mightily close at Silverstone and had it not been for a massive crash, only his second of the season, at Brands Hatch in free practice, he may well have done so at the final round. Despite a badly damaged finger, he still was challenging and despite not claiming any silverware, Bridewell, if nothing else, made a lot of his doubters eat their words.

**Results**

| | | | |
|---|---|---|---|
| Position: | 6 | | |
| Points: | 57 | | |
| Qualifying Poles: | | | |
| Fastest Lap Poles: | | | |
| Front Rows: | | | |
| Best Grid: | Po | | |
| Races: | 2 | | |
| Wins: | | | |
| Podiums: | | | |
| Best Result: | 4 | | |
| Fastest Laps: | | | |
| | | | |
| Brands Hatch Indy: | 6th | | |
| Thruxton: | 11th | 16th | |
| Oulton Park: | 5th | 7th | 5 |
| Snetterton: | 6th | C | |
| Knockhill: | 5th | 6th | |
| Oulton Park: | 6th | 7th | 8 |
| Brands Hatch GP: | 5th | 7th | |
| Cadwell Park: | 9th | 5th | |
| Donington Park: | 9th | 4th | |
| TT Circuit Assen: | 6th | 5th | |
| Silverstone: | 6th | 4th | |
| Brands Hatch GP: | 7th | 5th | 4 |

# James Westmoreland
## Team WFR

A little bit like Tommy Bridewell, James did everything but score a podium, however, unlike Tommy and team-mate Alex Lowes, the quietly-spoken Humbersider didn't quite have enough in his armoury to make it into the Showdown. Looking back, Westy did OK and with just three non-scores in his points tally, fully warranted his place as best of the rest with winning the BSB Riders' Cup. Indeed, he played a key part in helping Lowes' bid as he took vital points off Showdown hopefuls and was within a second of claiming that elusive podium spot in the first race of the Brands Hatch finale.

**Results**

| | | | |
|---|---|---|---|
| Position: | 7th | | |
| Points: | 182 | | |
| Qualifying Poles: | 0 | | |
| Fastest Lap Poles: | 0 | | |
| Front Rows: | 5 | | |
| Best Grid: | 3rd | | |
| Races: | 26 | | |
| Wins: | 0 | | |
| Podiums: | 0 | | |
| Best Result: | 4th | | |
| Fastest Laps: | 0 | | |
| | | | |
| Brands Hatch Indy: | 8th | | |
| Thruxton: | 9th | 9th | |
| Oulton Park: | 10th | 14th | 16th |
| Snetterton: | 12th | 9th | |
| Knockhill: | 11th | 5th | |
| Oulton Park: | 5th | 11th | 9th |
| Brands Hatch GP: | C | 10th | |
| Cadwell Park: | 8th | 6th | |
| Donington Park: | 5th | 6th | |
| TT Circuit Assen: | 8th | 8th | |
| Silverstone: | 5th | 9th | |
| Brands Hatch GP: | 4th | C | 6th |

# Noriyuki Haga
## Swan Yamaha

### Results

| | | | |
|---|---|---|---|
| Position: | | | 8th |
| Points: | | | 160 |
| Qualifying Poles: | | | 0 |
| Fastest Lap Poles: | | | 1 |
| Front Rows: | | | 4 |
| Best Grid: | | | Pole |
| Races: | | | 24 |
| Wins: | | | 0 |
| Podiums: | | | 1 |
| Best Result: | | | 2nd |
| Fastest Laps: | | | 0 |
| | | | |
| Brands Hatch Indy: | 13th | | |
| Thruxton: | R | 10th | |
| Oulton Park: | 2nd | 13th | 6th |
| Snetterton: | 4th | C | |
| Knockhill: | 6th | C | |
| Oulton Park: | 4th | 5th | 4th |
| Brands Hatch GP: | C | 5th | |
| Cadwell Park: | Inj | Inj | |
| Donington Park: | 21st | 12th | |
| TT Circuit Assen: | 5th | 6th | |
| Silverstone: | 16th | 15th | |
| Brands Hatch GP: | 8th | 9th | 10th |

As a rider of such pedigree, it would be all too easy to say that Nitro Nori bombed big style in what is probably his swansong season and when you examine the facts, perhaps he did, but there is a little more to it. Yes, three silly crashes at Snetterton, Knockhill and Brands thwarted his chances but there was the nasty collarbone injury he sustained at Cadwell which also added to the fact he didn't make the cut. New tracks, a new culture, the British weather and a change of crew chief all conspired against a rider who has won 43 WSB races and whereas the Japanese ace can still be petulant, he simply discovered that BSB is one tough cookie and even a rider of his class had his work cut out.

# Chris Walker
## Pr1mo Bournemouth Kawasaki

What more can you say about The Stalker? He simply keeps coming back for more and every year throws up a surprise. Only this season, it was the biggest one to date when he rolled the clock back and slithered his way to his first BSB victory in over a decade to become the fifth different winner in as many races. But in typical Walker fashion, just when it looked as if things were looking up, he got slapped back down and two broken heels at Knockhill saw his hopes of bettering his four BSB runner-up placings dashed. He battled on yet couldn't quite find the form of that day at Oulton but a top ten in BSB isn't a shabby achievement by anyone's imagination.

### Results

| | | | |
|---|---|---|---|
| Position: | | | 9th |
| Points: | | | 138 |
| Qualifying Poles: | | | 0 |
| Fastest Lap Poles: | | | 0 |
| Front Rows: | | | 1 |
| Best Grid: | | | 2nd |
| Races: | | | 26 |
| Wins: | | | 1 |
| Podiums: | | | 0 |
| Best Result: | | | 1st |
| Fastest Laps: | | | 0 |
| | | | |
| Brands Hatch Indy: | 12th | | |
| Thruxton: | R | 15th | |
| Oulton Park: | 7th | 1st | 9th |
| Snetterton: | 7th | 7th | |
| Knockhill: | R | R | |
| Oulton Park: | 7th | 12th | 11th |
| Brands Hatch GP: | 6th | C | |
| Cadwell Park: | 13th | 11th | |
| Donington Park: | 8th | 10th | |
| TT Circuit Assen: | 15th | 14th | |
| Silverstone: | 10th | 8th | |
| Brands Hatch GP: | R | R | 9th |

# Stuart Easton
## Rapid Solicitors Kawasaki

For a rider who, just the season before, sustained life-threatening injuries, Easton's top ten placing must rank as simply remarkable. Nowhere near bike fit at the start of the year, Stuart amazed everyone by challenging for a podium in round two at Thruxton which eventually came the next time out at Oulton. But just as it looked as if he may challenge for a Showdown place, lady luck intervened when an infection on some of the metalwork used to rebuild his shattered limbs ruled the Scot out of his home round at Knockhill and injury at a non-championship race saw him miss more races. It wasn't to be but it was the bravest performance of the year without doubt.

### Results

| | | | |
|---|---|---|---|
| Position: | | | 10th |
| Points: | | | 135 |
| Qualifying Poles: | | | 0 |
| Fastest Lap Poles: | | | 0 |
| Front Rows: | | | 1 |
| Best Grid: | | | 3rd |
| Races: | | | 21 |
| Wins: | | | 0 |
| Podiums: | | | 2 |
| Best Result: | | | 3rd |
| Fastest Laps: | | | 0 |
| | | | |
| Brands Hatch Indy: | R | | |
| Thruxton: | 5th | 4th | |
| Oulton Park: | 9th | 5th | 3rd |
| Snetterton: | R | 8th | |
| Knockhill: | NS | NS | |
| Oulton Park: | Inj | Inj | Inj |
| Brands Hatch GP: | 8th | F | |
| Cadwell Park: | 19th | 14th | |
| Donington Park: | 4th | 7th | |
| TT Circuit Assen: | 9th | 10th | |
| Silverstone: | R | R | |
| Brands Hatch GP: | 5th | 7th | 12th |

| | | | | | |
|---|---|---|---|---|---|
| 1st | Finishing Position | R | Retired | NS | Non Starter |
| C | Crashed | Inj. | Injured | Dq | Disqualified |

# Rapid Solicitors Kawasaki

# Rapid Solicitors Kawasaki

**Machinery:** Kawasaki ZX-10R
**Principal:** Paul Bird
**Located:** Penrith, Cumbria
**Pedigree:** British Superbike champions 2002, 2003 & 2012
**Website:** www.pbmuk.net

Double BSB champion Shane Byrne took the lead in the title race for the first time at Silverstone and cemented his and the Penrith-based team's third BSB title with a resounding triple victory at his local Brands Hatch track in the final round and in doing so, emerged unbeaten in his last seven races around the Kent GP track. Following on from serious injuries last year, it was always going to be a tough ask for team-mate Stuart Easton but he showed the odd glimpse of form this season, including a podium at Oulton Park.

### Shane Byrne

| | |
|---|---|
| Number: | 67 |
| Nickname: | Shakey |
| Lives: | Lambeth, London |
| DOB: | 12 October 1976 |
| First BSB Race: | Silverstone 1999 |
| BSB Races: | 219 |
| BSB Wins: | 41 |
| Honours: | Triple MCE BSB champion 2003, 2008 & 2012 |

### Stuart Easton

| | |
|---|---|
| Number: | 3 |
| Nickname: | - |
| Lives: | Hawick, Scotland |
| DOB: | 21 July 1983 |
| First BSB Race: | Silverstone 2004 |
| BSB Races: | 107 |
| BSB Wins: | 3 |
| Honours: | British Supersport champion 2002, three Macau GP wins |

**Other rider: Keith Farmer**

Teams: Rapid Solicitors Kawasaki

Tyco Suzuki

# Tyco Suzuki

**Machinery:** Suzuki GSX-R1000
**Manager:** Philip Neill
**Located:** Moneymore, Northern Ireland
**Pedigree:** British Supersport & Superstock champions
**Website:** www.tyco-suzuki.co.uk

The only rider to have scored points in every BSB round meant consistency was the key for Josh Brookes who was leading the title chase after Assen. But results at Silverstone could have been better and he had to play second fiddle to Byrne at Brands Hatch to end up as runner-up so the Aussie will have to wait at least another year for his chance. Team-mate and 2011 Supersport champion Alastair Seeley started the season brightly at Brands Hatch on the podium but then it seemed to go downhill rapidly for the wee Ulsterman.

| Josh Brookes | |
|---|---|
| Number: | 2 |
| Nickname: | Brookesy |
| Lives: | Sydney, Australia |
| DOB: | 28 April 1983 |
| First BSB Race: | Brands Hatch 2009 |
| BSB Races: | 94 |
| BSB Wins: | 11 |
| Honours: | Double Australian champion |

| Alastair Seeley | |
|---|---|
| Number: | 34 |
| Nickname: | The Wizard |
| Lives: | Carrickfergus, Northern Ireland |
| DOB: | 4 October 1979 |
| First BSB Race: | Brands Hatch 2009 |
| BSB Races: | 57 |
| BSB Wins: | 1 |
| Honours: | British Supersport and National Superstock 1000 champion |

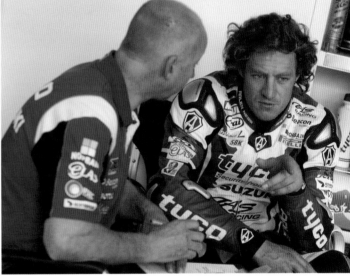

# Swan Yamaha

# Swan Yamaha

**Machinery:** Yamaha YZR-R1
**Principal:** Shaun Muir
**Located:** Guisborough, Cleveland
**Pedigree:** 2011 MCE British Superbike champions
**Website:** www.swanyamaha.co.uk

Despite winning the most races going into the Showdown and leading the title chase, it all turned sour for defending BSB champion Tommy Hill when a freak accident on the grid at Assen left him with a mountain to climb. Hill fought all the way to the end but couldn't do enough to keep his faint title hopes alive and ended up third. As for multiple WSB race winner 'Nitro' Noriyuki Haga, it was a tough season and he never really seemed to get to grips with things, scoring only one podium on his way to eighth in the final standings.

| Tommy Hill | |
| --- | --- |
| Number: | 1 |
| Nickname: | - |
| Lives: | Lingfield, Surrey |
| DOB: | 9 February 1985 |
| First BSB Race: | Silverstone 2004 |
| BSB Races: | 187 |
| BSB Wins: | 19 |
| Honours: | 2011 MCE British Superbike champion |

| Noriyuki Haga | |
| --- | --- |
| Number: | 41 |
| Nickname: | Nitro Nori |
| Lives: | Nagoya, Japan |
| DOB: | 2 March 1975 |
| First BSB Race: | Oulton Park 2004 |
| BSB Races: | 27 |
| BSB Wins: | 0 |
| Honours: | Runner-up World Superbike Championship 2000, 2007, 2009 |

# Samsung Honda

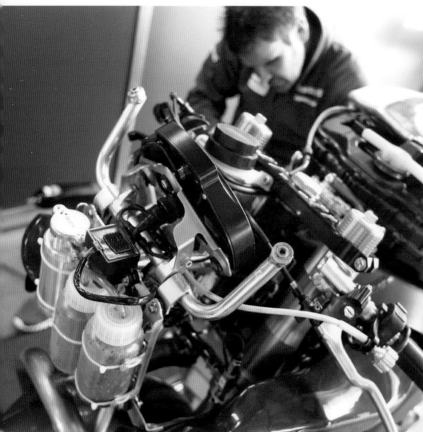

# Samsung Honda

**Machinery:** Honda CBR1000RR Fireblade
**Manager:** Xavier Beltran
**Located:** Louth, Lincolnshire
**Pedigree:** British Superbike champions 2006, 2007 & 2010
**Website:** www.honda-racing.co.uk

Once again, the Showdown wasn't kind to Michael Laverty, which mirrored the two years previous and his challenge faded out. Tyre and set-up woes haunted the Ulsterman at times during the season and they came back with a vengeance at both Assen and Silverstone. His season didn't get going until mid season, which was too late, and although he did manage a couple of wins, it wasn't enough. Team-mate Jon Kirkham started the season brightly with a victory at Brands Hatch but his challenge faded following a huge crash at Oulton Park in May.

### Michael Laverty

| | |
|---|---|
| Number: | 7 |
| Nickname: | Choo Choo |
| Lives: | Toome, Co. Antrim, Northern Ireland |
| DOB: | 7 June 1981 |
| First BSB Race: | Brands Hatch 2005 |
| BSB Races: | 144 |
| BSB Wins: | 7 |
| Honours: | British Supersport 2007 |

### Jon Kirkham

| | |
|---|---|
| Number: | 10 |
| Nickname: | JK |
| Lives: | Ockbrook, Derbyshire |
| DOB: | 16 November 1984 |
| First BSB Race: | Silverstone 2003 |
| BSB Races: | 161 |
| BSB Wins: | 2 |
| Honours: | 2011 National Superstock 1000 champion |

# MSS Bathams
# Kawasaki

# MSS Bathams Kawasaki

**Machinery:** Kawasaki ZX-10R
**Principal:** Nick Morgan
**Located:** Colchester, Essex
**Pedigree:** MCE British Superbike podium finishers
**Website:** www.msscolchesterkawasaki.com

It's was a mega-tough season for Nick Morgan's team although there was the odd glimpse of go
fortune along the way. Michael Rutter got the season off to a great start with a podium at Bran
Hatch and mid-season signing Danny Buchan was singularly impressive at Cadwell Park with a f
fourth place but other than that, there was little joy. The combination of the experienced Rutter, w
nearly 400 MCE BSB starts to his name, and the exciting prospect of Buchan could well be one
watch in 2013 if they are retained.

## Michael Rutter

| | |
|---|---|
| Number: | 4 |
| Nickname: | Blade |
| Lives: | Bridgnorth, Shropshire |
| DOB: | 18 April 1972 |
| First BSB Race: | Donington Park, April 1995 |
| BSB Races: | 396 |
| BSB Wins: | 28 |
| Honours: | Twice runner-up MCE British Superbike Championship. TT, NW200 & Macau GP winner |

## Danny Buchan

| | |
|---|---|
| Number: | 8 |
| Nickname: | Boom Boo |
| Lives: | Basildon, Esse |
| DOB: | 28 April 199 |
| First BSB Race: | Brands Hatch 20 |
| BSB Races: | |
| BSB Wins: | |
| Honours: | Twice Runner-up Metzeler Nation Superstock Championship |

**Other rider:** Peter Hickman

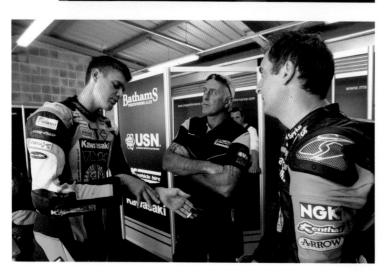

**Buildbase BMW Motorrad**

# Buildbase
# BMW Motorrad

**Machinery:** BMW S1000RR
**Principal:** Stuart Hicken
**Located:** Peggs Green, Leicestershire
**Pedigree:** British Superbike race winners
**Website:** www.buildbasebmw.co.uk

Stuart Hicken's team started the season strongly but a couple of subsequent crashes and injuries put paid to their chances early on. Barry Burrell showed good pace initially before a mid season dip but he bounced back in superb fashion to run at the front at the final meeting at Brands Hatch, just missing out on a podium. Team-mate Peter Hickman, who came into the team mid season to replace Dan Linfoot, worked wonders on his short time on the BMW and had he had a full season, would have been much higher up the table.

| Peter Hickman | |
|---|---|
| Number: | 60 |
| Nickname: | Hicky |
| Lives: | Louth, Lincolnshire |
| DOB: | 8 April 1987 |
| First BSB Race: | Brands Hatch 2006 |
| BSB Races: | 145 |
| BSB Wins: | 0 |
| Honours: | National Superstock Cup champion 2004 |

| Barry Burrell | |
|---|---|
| Number: | 77 |
| Nickname: | Bazza |
| Lives: | Bishop Auckland, Co. Durham |
| DOB: | 14 August 1985 |
| First BSB Race: | Brands Hatch 2011 |
| BSB Races: | 52 |
| BSB Wins: | 0 |
| Honours: | 3rd 2011 BSB-EVO Championship |

**Other rider: Dan Linfoot**

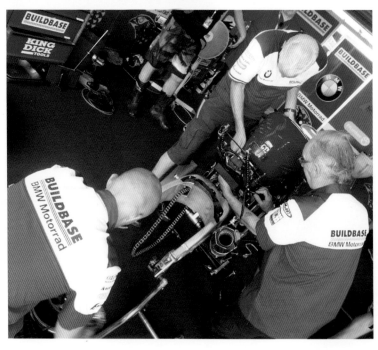

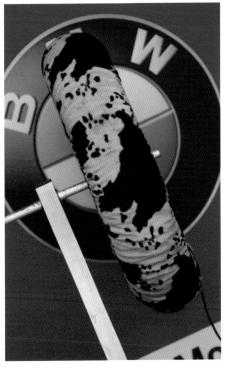

Tweet like a bird?
Follow me on twitter
@peterhickman60

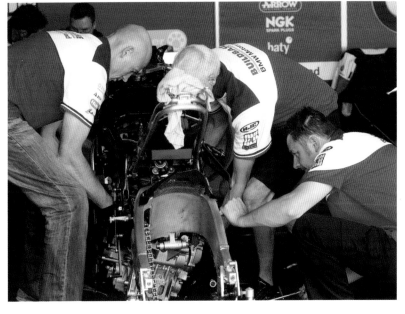

# Team WFR Honda

**Machinery:** Honda CBR1000RR Fireblade
**Owner:** Miles Schofield
**Located:** Ossett, West Yorkshire
**Pedigree:** BSB-EVO champions 2011
**Website:** www.teamwfr.co.uk

Over the final four rounds, Alex Lowes was simply sensational and despite being the last rider to qualify for the Showdown, he ended up being the dark horse to win this year's BSB crown. Pole position and two podiums at Assen were backed up with a fantastic double at Silverstone but three DNFs at Brands Hatch scuppered his chances in the end. James Westmoreland showed good pace to hold seventh in the standings and lifted the BSB Riders Cup as third team member Graeme Gowland quit mid way through the season.

| Alex Lowes | |
|---|---|
| Number: | 22 |
| Nickname: | - |
| Lives: | Saxilby, Lincolnshire |
| DOB: | 14 September 1990 |
| First BSB Race: | Oulton Park 2010 |
| BSB Races: | 52 |
| BSB Wins: | 2 |
| Honours: | BSB wins and World championship experience |

| James Westmoreland | |
|---|---|
| Number: | 27 |
| Nickname: | Westy |
| Lives: | Beverley, East Yorkshire |
| DOB: | 24 June 1988 |
| First BSB Race: | Brands Hatch 2011 |
| BSB Races: | 49 |
| BSB Wins: | 0 |
| Honours: | Three times British Supersport Championship runner-up |

| Other rider: Graeme Gowland |
|---|

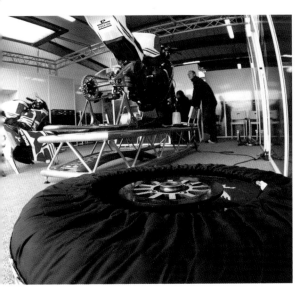

# Splitlath-Redmond Racing Aprilia

# Splitlath-Redmond Racing Aprilia

**Machinery:** Aprilia RSV4
**Principals:** John Dimbylow & Derek Redmond
**Located:** Hay on Wye, Powys
**Pedigree:** Runners-up in BSB-EVO 2010
**Website:** www.splitlathredmond.com

After persevering with John Laverty and Florian Marino for half the season, it was then all change in the team owned jointly by former Olympic athlete Derek Redmond and John Dimbylow. Experienced World Superbike star Mark Aitchison came into the squad at Cadwell before being injured and was joined at Assen by Jakub Smrz who proved a revelation only to be denied a good result due to technical problems. Troy Herfoss also had a brief spell on the bike as the team eventually unearthed the RSV4's undoubted potential.

### Mark Aitchison

| | |
|---|---|
| Number: | 18 |
| Nickname: | Atcho |
| Lives: | Gosford, Australia |
| DOB: | 22 November 1983 |
| First BSB Race: | Oulton Park 2012 |
| BSB Races: | 7 |
| BSB Wins: | 0 |
| Honours: | 5th European Superstock Championship 2007 |

### Jakub Smrz

| | |
|---|---|
| Number: | 96 |
| Nickname: | Kuba |
| Lives: | Ceske Budejovice, Czech Republic |
| DOB: | 7 April 1983 |
| First BSB Race: | Assen 2012 |
| BSB Races: | 7 |
| BSB Wins: | 0 |
| Honours: | 4 times World Superbike Championship podiums |

**Other riders: John Laverty, Florian Marino, Troy Herfoss**

**Padgetts Racing**

# Padgetts Racing

**Machinery:** Honda CBR1000RR Fireblade
**Principal:** Clive Padgett
**Located:** Batley, West Yorkshire
**Pedigree:** British champions & Grand Prix experience
**Website:** www.padgetts-racing.co.uk

2012 was a mixed season for the experienced Yorkshire team who started the season in impressive form as Ulsterman Ian Lowry led the title race early on courtesy of a strong start which included a win at Thruxton. A number of confidence-sapping crashes saw Lowry drop down the order and he left the team prior to the final round where he was replaced by Samsung Honda's Superstock rider, Jason O Halloran. Italian team-mate Luca Scassa didn't have the best of luck either but was resurgent at both Donington and Assen although he and the team were expecting better.

## Ian Lowry

| | |
|---|---:|
| Number: | 5 |
| Nickname: | - |
| Lives: | Moira, Co. Down, Northern Ireland |
| DOB: | 22 September 1986 |
| First BSB Race: | Brands Hatch 2009 |
| BSB Races: | 77 |
| BSB Wins: | 1 |
| Honours: | Runner-up British Supersport Championship 2007 |

## Luca Scassa

| | |
|---|---:|
| Number: | 99 |
| Nickname: | The Rocker |
| Lives: | Arezzo, Italy |
| DOB: | 23 August 1983 |
| First BSB Race: | Brands Hatch 2012 |
| BSB Races: | 25 |
| BSB Wins: | 0 |
| Honours: | 2008 Italian Superbike champion |

**Other riders:** Jason O'Halloran

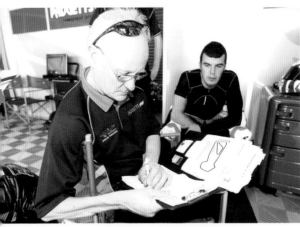

# Supersonic BMW
# Racing Team

# Supersonic BMW Racing Team

**Machinery:** BMW S1000RR
**Principal:** Danilo Soncini
**Located:** Dalmine, Italy
**Pedigree:** World Superbike Championship experience
**Website:** www.supersonicracingteam.com

Tommy Bridewell and the Italians were the fairytale story of BSB 2012 as the rookie team with the rider they signed just days before the season opener at Brands Hatch qualified for the Showdown. The fact that Bridewell didn't score a podium didn't really matter in the end as taking pole position and leading the race at Silverstone made up for it, and had it not been for a nasty finger injury at the last round, he may well have claimed the elusive silverware. Team-mate Patric Muff also impressed this season and got quicker each time out on the BMW.

| Patric Muff | |
|---|---|
| Number: | 24 |
| Nickname: | - |
| Lives: | Bannwil, Switzerland |
| DOB: | 24 September 1983 |
| First BSB Race: | Brands Hatch 2011 |
| BSB Races: | 52 |
| BSB Wins: | 0 |
| Honours: | Swiss Superstock 1000 champion |

| Tommy Bridewell | |
|---|---|
| Number: | 46 |
| Nickname: | - |
| Lives: | Devizes, Wiltshire |
| DOB: | 4 August 1988 |
| First BSB Race: | Brands Hatch 2007 |
| BSB Races: | 98 |
| BSB Wins: | 0 |
| Honours: | Runner-up Virgin Mobile Cup 2005 |

# Moto Rapido Racing Ducati

**Machinery:** Ducati 1199 Panigale
**Manager:** Steve Moore
**Located:** Winchester, Hampshire
**Pedigree:** Race winners in BSB-EVO
**Website:** www.motorapido.co.uk

British ace Scott Smart and the first Saudi Arabian to race in BSB, Abdulaziz Binladin campaigned the Moto Rapido Panigales this season as they continued their long-term association with Ducati. Former 250cc British champion and BSB race winner Smart showed the potential of the bike at various points during the season but Binladen was injured at Cadwell Park and struggled to recover. Ducati test rider Matteo Baiocco deputised at Silverstone and helped with development as the team looks to 2013.

## Abdulaziz Binladen

| | |
|---|---|
| Number: | 36 |
| Nickname: | Aladdin |
| Lives: | Jeddah, Saudi Arabia |
| DOB: | 26 November 1981 |
| First BSB Race: | Brands Hatch 2012 |
| BSB Races: | 16 |
| BSB Wins: | 0 |
| Honours: | Twice UAE Superbike champion |

## Scott Smart

| | |
|---|---|
| Number: | 88 |
| Nickname: | Smart Arse |
| Lives: | Maidstone, Kent |
| DOB: | 29 May 1972 |
| First BSB Race: | Silverstone 2003 |
| BSB Races: | 188 |
| BSB Wins: | 4 |
| Honours: | Superteen and 250cc British champion |

**Other rider: Matteo Baiocco**

# Quattro Plant Kawasaki Superbike Team

**Machinery:** Kawasaki ZX-10R
**Manager:** John Jameson
**Located:** Liverpool
**Pedigree:** British Superbike Cup champions 2006
**Website:** www.pr-racing.co.uk

After a difficult first half of the season with Freddy Foray and Gary Mason, a change in personnel saw former triple British Supersport champion Karl Harris drafted into the team and his arrival at Cadwell Park was simply stunning. 'Bomber' looked to carry that form into Donington Park but a wrist injury ruled him out and he never really recaptured the same form after that. Australian Nick Waters was the latest addition to ride for the team and partnered Harris for the final meeting having enjoyed success back home this year.

| Nick Waters | |
| --- | --- |
| Number: | 52 |
| Nickname: | - |
| Lives: | Mildura, Australia |
| DOB: | 27 October 1993 |
| First BSB Race: | Brands Hatch 2012 |
| BSB Races: | 3 |
| BSB Wins: | 0 |
| Honours: | Podiums in Australian Supersport Championship |

| Karl Harris | |
| --- | --- |
| Number: | 68 |
| Nickname: | Bomber |
| Lives: | Sheffield |
| DOB: | 21 October 1979 |
| First BSB Race: | Brands Hatch, 2000 |
| BSB Races: | 162 |
| BSB Wins: | 0 |
| Honours: | Three-times British Supersport champion |

**Other riders: Gary Mason, Freddy Foray, Mark Aitchison, Tom Grant**

Teams: Quattro Plant Kawasaki Superbike Team

# Pr1mo Bournmouth Kawasaki Racing

**Machinery:** Kawasaki ZX-10R
**Manager:** Peter Extance
**Located:** Bournemouth, Dorset
**Pedigree:** BSB race winners
**Website:** www.bournemouthkawasakiracing.co.uk

Veteran Chris Walker showed that he's still very much a force to be reckoned with as he enjoyed something of a renaissance this season much to the delight of his legions of fans. 'The Stalker' took his first MCE BSB victory since 2000 at Oulton Park back in May but following injury he couldn't just manage to squeeze himself into the Showdown but battled right to the end to finish an impressive ninth. James Hillier rode for the first half of the season but was injured at Knockhill and John Laverty came into the team for the final few rounds and looked good after returning this season from serious injury.

| Chris Walker | |
| --- | --- |
| Number: | 9 |
| Nickname: | Stalker |
| Lives: | Newark, Nottinghamshire |
| DOB: | 25 March 1972 |
| First BSB Race: | Donington Park, 1996 |
| BSB Races: | 233 |
| BSB Wins: | 21 |
| Honours: | Four times MCE British Superbike runner-up |

| John Laverty | |
| --- | --- |
| Number: | 14 |
| Nickname: | J-Lav |
| Lives: | Toome, Co. Antrim, Northern Ireland |
| DOB: | 06 July 1982 |
| First BSB Race: | Brands Hatch 2007 |
| BSB Races: | 110 |
| BSB Wins: | 0 |
| Honours: | British Superbike Cup champion 2008 |

**Other riders: James Hillier, Gary Mason, Victor Cox**

# Doodson Motorsport

**Machinery:** Honda CBR1000RR Fireblade
**Team Owner:** Tom Tunstall
**Located:** Huddersfield, West Yorkshire
**Pedigree:** World Championship experience
**Website:** www.tomtunstall.co.uk

After starting the season on the new Ducati Panigale, the experienced team returned to Honda power mid season. The venerable Fireblades on which Tom Tunstall has contested BSB in the past were converted to the new 2012 regulations and following injury to original teamster David Anthony in July, in came former Grand Prix and World Supersport ace Robbin Harms to take up the challenge. Whereas Tunstall suffered with problems, Harms was mightily impressive and scored the team's best results at Assen.

## Tom Tunstall

| | |
|---|---|
| Number: | 21 |
| Nickname: | - |
| Lives: | Huddersfield, West Yorkshire |
| DOB: | 21 June 1978 |
| First BSB Race: | April 2007 |
| BSB Races: | 133 |
| BSB Wins: | 0 |
| Honours: | 14 years British and three years World championship experience |

## Robbin Harms

| | |
|---|---|
| Number: | 127 |
| Nickname: | - |
| Lives: | Copenhagen, Denmark |
| DOB: | 09 June 1981 |
| First BSB Race: | Cadwell Park, 2012 |
| BSB Races: | 10 |
| BSB Wins: | 0 |
| Honours: | 5th 2006 World Supersport Championship |

**Other riders: Alex Polita, David Anthony**

# Hardinge Sorrymate.com Honda

**Machinery:** Honda CBR1000RR Fireblade
**Owner:** Jenny Tinmouth
**Located:** Ellesmere Port, Cheshire
**Pedigree:** Debut Season in MCE BSB
**Website:** www.twowheelracing.co.uk

After a tough start, the world's fastest lady road racer who runs her own team used 2012 to gain more and more experience aboard the Honda Fireblade. It was very much a learning year and although Jenny didn't manage to squeeze into the points this season, she finished most races and certainly didn't disgrace herself. And the good news is she's planning on racing again in BSB next year!

| Jenny Tinmouth | |
|---|---|
| Number: | 8 |
| Nickname: | - |
| Lives: | Ellesmere Port, Cheshire |
| DOB: | 03 August 1979 |
| First BSB Race: | Croft 2011 |
| BSB Races: | 26 |
| BSB Wins: | 0 |
| Honours: | British Supersport Cup podiums, fastest lady TT rider |

# GBmoto Racing Honda

**Machinery:** Honda CBR1000RR Fireblade
**Principal:** Mark Smith-Halvorsen
**Located:** Godstone, Surrey
**Pedigree:** Debut season in MCE British Superbike Championship
**Website:** www.gbmoto.com

The debut team in BSB started with a front row placing for Tristan Palmer at Brands Hatch at Easter but that was about as good as it got this season. The team then scored their first points of the season at round three at Oulton Park with Luke Quigley. After that it was a tough battle for both Palmer and Quigley, both of whom suffered injuries at various points during the season to thwart their bid for honours.

| Tristan Palmer | |
| --- | --- |
| Number: | 33 |
| Nickname: | Treacle |
| Lives: | Nuneaton, Warwickshire |
| DOB: | 17 August 1982 |
| First BSB Race: | Brands Hatch 2005 |
| BSB Races: | 117 |
| BSB Wins: | 0 |
| Honours: | British Superbike Cup champion 2007 |

| Luke Quigley | |
| --- | --- |
| Number: | 51 |
| Nickname: | Wriggly |
| Lives: | Dudley, West Midlands |
| DOB: | 23 January 1979 |
| First BSB Race: | Croft 2005 |
| BSB Races: | 56 |
| BSB Wins: | 0 |
| Honours: | 3rd National Superstock 1000 Championship 2003, 2006 & 2011 |

# MSVR

## SOLE TYRE SUPPLIER AND ASSOCIATE SPONSOR

Pirelli proudly continues its sole tyre supply agreement with the British
Superbike Championship as the series goes from strength to strength. The
legendary Italian marque has been the sole tyre supplier for this prestigious
series from 2008 and will continue until 2015 under the current term.

With the 2012 Championship rule changes and supply of the Diablo
Superbike control tyre, the BSB Paddock saw a new level of equality with
eight different race winners. Pirelli Diablo Supercorsa 'DOT treaded' tyres
are used in the more production based Supersport 600 and Ducati 848
Challenge support classes.

All Pirelli tyres used in all classes can also be bought over the counter for
racers of all levels and trackday riders, staying true to Pirelli's motto
"We sell what we race, we race what we sell."

Pirelli UK's Marketing Manager Jim Worland explained, "The British
Superbike Championship is one of the most prestigious and popular
motorcycle race series in the World and our technicians are very interested
in our feedback from these 'over the counter' production tyres. This real
world race R+D directly develops our race and road tyres and improves
the knowledge base of our engineers. We look forward to another thrilling
installment of the BSB success story in 2013!"

pirelli.co.uk/moto

**POWER IS NOTHING WITHOUT CONTROL**

# RACE ROAD

## RACE = ROAD. SBK TECHNOLOGY FOR EVERYDAY ROADS.

ROSSO GENERATION. A range of products derived from Pirelli's experience in the Superbike World Championship, that offers the best in terms of performance and innovation. Discover the new DIABLO ROSSO II, the ultimate bi-compound tyre for pure road use that combines sporty character, versatility and confidence in any riding condition. And the DIABLO ROSSO Corsa delivers Diablo Family emotions to satisfy racetrack adrenaline, whilst providing every day riding assurance. Rosso Generation tyres can be personalised by applying sidewall labels you can create online using logos and customised text, making your tyres truly unique.

DIABLO ROSSO and POWER IS NOTHING WITHOUT CONTROL are trademarks of Pirelli Tyre Spa.

**DIABLO**
ROSSO II

**POWER IS NOTHING WITHOUT CONTROL**

# Circuit Maps

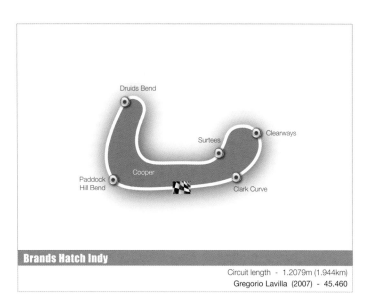

## Brands Hatch Indy

Circuit length - 1.2079m (1.944km)
Gregorio Lavilla (2007) - 45.460

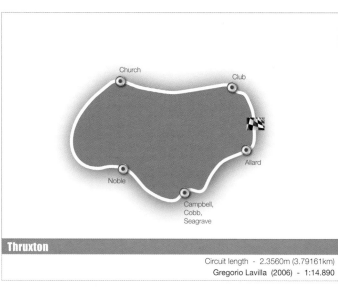

## Thruxton

Circuit length - 2.3560m (3.79161km)
Gregorio Lavilla (2006) - 1:14.890

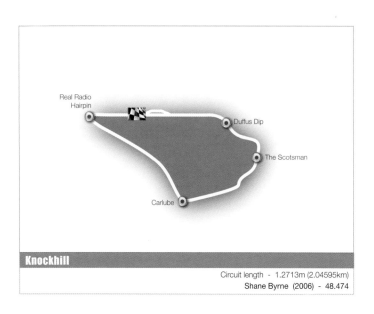

## Knockhill

Circuit length - 1.2713m (2.04595km)
Shane Byrne (2006) - 48.474

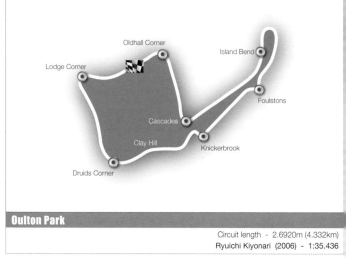

## Oulton Park

Circuit length - 2.6920m (4.332km)
Ryuichi Kiyonari (2006) - 1:35.436

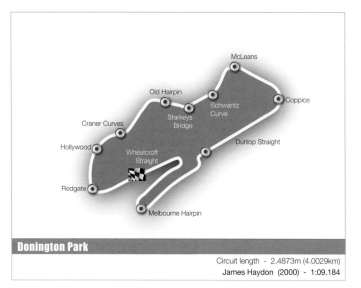

## Donington Park

Circuit length - 2.4873m (4.0029km)
James Haydon (2000) - 1:09.184

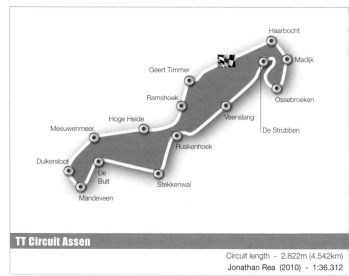

## TT Circuit Assen

Circuit length - 2.822m (4.542km)
Jonathan Rea (2010) - 1:36.312

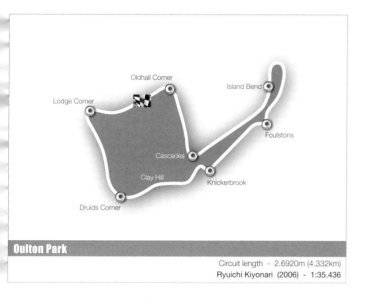

**Oulton Park**

Circuit length - 2.6920m (4.332km)
Ryuichi Kiyonari (2006) - 1:35.436

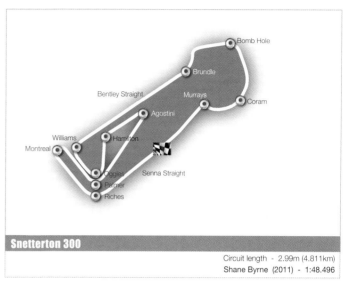

**Snetterton 300**

Circuit length - 2.99m (4.811km)
Shane Byrne (2011) - 1:48.496

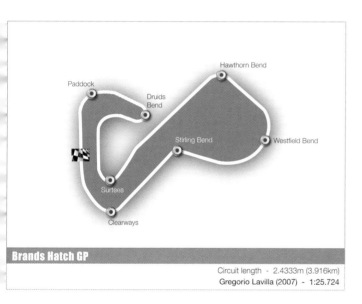

**Brands Hatch GP**

Circuit length - 2.4333m (3.916km)
Gregorio Lavilla (2007) - 1:25.724

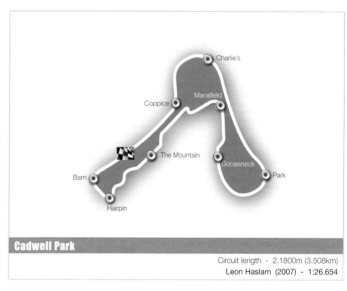

**Cadwell Park**

Circuit length - 2.1800m (3.508km)
Leon Haslam (2007) - 1:26.654

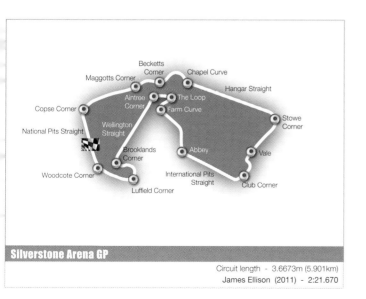

**Silverstone Arena GP**

Circuit length - 3.6673m (5.901km)
James Ellison (2011) - 2:21.670

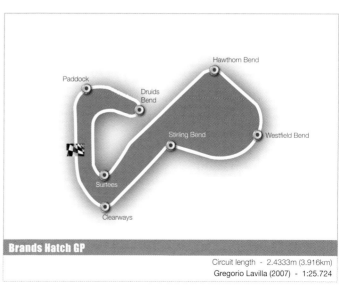

**Brands Hatch GP**

Circuit length - 2.4333m (3.916km)
Gregorio Lavilla (2007) - 1:25.724

**01**

# Brands Hatch Indy

06 - 09 APRIL 2012

**Top left:** Japanese WSB ace Noryuki Haga arrived at BSB with big expectations as Tommy Hill's title defence got off to a less than satisfactory start

**Below:** James Westmoreland made a solid start as did Michael Rutter on the MSS Kawasaki (bottom right)

**Top left:** Luca Scassa was stylish on the Padgetts Honda as was Alex Lowes (right)

**Below:** Splitlath Redmond started the season with Florian Marino while eventual champion Shane Byrne (right) took only nine points away from round one

**Left:** Byrne and Josh Brookes gave a taste of things to come as they battled closely

**Below:** Paddock Hill chaos as Graeme Gowland and Florian Marino crash out in spectacular fashion

**Bottom left:** Shakey leads the pack into Druids but **(bottom right)** Jon Kirkham and Alastair Seeley left Brands at the top of the pile

# Brands Hatch Indy

## FIRST BLOOD TO KIRKHAM...

Jon Kirkham enjoyed the perfect debut with the Samsung Honda team as he fully exploited a minor error by Alastair Seeley aboard the Tyco Suzuki on the exit of Clark Curve to take the opening round victory which, due to a combination of rain and fluids spilt on the circuit by various tumbles, was the only Superbike race of the day.

Kirkham's team-mate Michael Laverty was among the fallers together with Swan Yamaha's Tommy Hill whose title defence began on a pointless note. The actual race action, featuring for the first time the 'back to basics' technical regulations that outlawed traction control and anti-wheelie devices, centred on a scrap for supremacy between Kirkham, Seeley and his team-mate Josh Brookes, and Michael Rutter aboard the Bathams MSS Kawasaki.

Seeley, revelling in the conditions, carved under Rutter at Paddock Hill Bend at two thirds distance and then two laps later was leading having nosed clear of Kirkham at Druids while Brookes who was upping the tempo held on somehow as his bike bucked out of line at Graham Hill dropping him back to tenth place.

It seemed the race was going Seeley's way but Kirkham was eager to double his winning tally in the top flight and he was closing in on the British Supersport title holder, ready to pounce when the opportunity came. And it did on the last lap as the back end of Seeley's bike slewed sideways, he lost drive momentarily and with it the race as Kirkham took the flag.

Rutter came in a solid third ahead of Padgetts Honda rider Ian Lowry with Gary Mason just behind from Tommy Bridewell who had signed a last minute deal to ride for the Supersonic BMW team that was making its debut into the British series. They were not the only newcomers as the buoyant championship attracted a number of international stars, among them World Endurance champion Freddie Foray, who ran ninth ahead of Brookes, and World Superbike legend Noriyuki Haga who was a further three places back.

In what can only be described as a race of attrition, with only 21 of the 33 starters finishing, it was a typically wet and chilly Easter Monday, not only for those used to warmer climes, but also for those seasoned regulars on the British scene.

| BSB CHAMPIONSHIP POINTS | | |
|---|---|---|
| 1 | KIRKHAM | 25 |
| 2 | SEELEY | 20 |
| 3 | RUTTER | 16 |
| 4 | LOWRY | 13 |
| 5 | MASON | 11 |
| 6 | BRIDEWELL | 10 |

☑ **EXHILARATING BIKES**
☑ **SENSATIONAL OFFER**
☐ **EXCITING ADVERT**

Well, two out of three ain't bad.

**0%APR**
REPRESENTATIVE
**OVER 42 MONTHS**

Honda Contact Centre: 0845 200 8000

www.honda.co.uk

02

Thruxton

13 - 15 April 2012

Left: Shakey had an average day by his standards but did manage to climb onto the rostrum with a third place in race two while right: Ian Lowry surprised a few people as he took the race one win and left Thruxton with the Championship lead

Top: Brookes was consistent as usual while (top right) Hickman struggled as did Easton

Right: As usual, Thruxton saw tight racing at the front

**Top left:** Although Seeley rode hard, he managed to take just one solitary point from the weekend

**Left:** Lowry was away like a scalded cat while the Samsung Hondas of Laverty and Kirkham struggled at the Hampshire circuit

# Thruxton

## LOWRY AND BROOKES CLEAN UP...

Ian Lowry and Josh Brookes were the race winners in Hampshire while Tommy Hill took some comfort for his opening round demise by racking up solid points and with them, some vital podium credits with a pair of hard earned second places ahead of first Brookes and then the former two times title winner Shane Byrne.

Former chef Lowry cooked up the biggest surprise of the afternoon as he converted his first BSB front row start into a maiden race win and he did it in style disposing of the threat of Swan Yamaha riding Hill by almost three seconds. It prompted a heavy mix of delight and embarrassment in the Padgetts Honda garage as the congratulations poured in from wide and far while team manager Clive Padgett found himself at the centre of the media spotlight, quipping: "This was not a bad result for a team of mates!"

It was always going to be a hard act for Lowry to follow and an error at the start of the second race left him playing catch up on the rest though he came through in fifth place and that was sufficient to put him at the top of the overall standings.

Brookes also had a fight on his hands as he scrapped to improve on his earlier third place. A poor start from the front row saw his Tyco Suzuki running in mid-pack in the early stages but the Aussie was full of fight, carving through to snatch the victory away from Hill on the final lap, though by little more than half a second in one of his greatest rides ever.

Hill, in common with a number of riders, struggled for grip in both races but rode well, leading both races before slipping back. Byrne, aboard the Rapid Solicitors Kawasaki, had similar problems, as did the Samsung Honda duo of Michael Laverty and Jon Kirkham while Stuart Easton, continuing his comeback from horrific injuries sustained the previous year in practice for the North West 200, took some satisfaction from his fifth and fourth place finishes.

Michael Rutter had been in the frame for a strong points haul but the radiator of his Bathams MSS Kawasaki was holed by a stone when he was well placed in the opener and then more overheating problems sidelined him next time out.

| BSB CHAMPIONSHIP POINTS | | |
|---|---|---|
| 1 | LOWRY | 49 |
| 2 | BROOKES | 47 |
| 3 | KIRKHAM | 43 |
| 4 | HILL | 40 |
| 5 | BYRNE | 38 |
| 6 | EASTON | 24 |

# 03 Oulton Park

05 - 07 MAY 2012

**Top left:** Haga returned to the scene of his infamous 'fireball' incident and showed promise with a race one podium but failed to match that result in either of the other two races

**Left:** Stuart Easton made one of his trademark starts as he heads the pack into turn one while Lowry (right) had a dismal follow up from his impressive Thruxton performance taking only three points from three races

**Top:** Josh Brookes put in a number of consistent rides on the Tyco Suzuki to consolidate his second place in the championship.

**Right:** The temperature didn't seem to affect Tommy Hill and he left Oulton heading the points table

**Below:** Josh Brookes may have an aggressive riding style, but is accurate nonetheless as he leads through Britten's

**Right:** Michael Laverty pushed hard

**Bottom right:** Shakey celebrates his race three win taking him to third in the Championship

NV400

# Oulton Park

## WALKER ROLLS BACK THE YEARS!

The technical regulations had been designed to create a level playing field with the action big on rider skill and they won high praise from Chris Walker, four times in previous years a runner-up in BSB, as he rode his Pr1mo Bournemouth Kawasaki to victory in the second of the three races being held at the Cheshire circuit.

It was a first victory in some 12 years for the 40-year-old Nottinghamshire rider and it was scored on a difficult drying circuit. Walker was running fourth on the opening lap but he was soon turning up the heat on Tommy Hill and then turning his attention to Josh Brookes who was hotly pursuing the race leading Shane Byrne. By half distance Walker was running second and reeling in Byrne, taking him at Lakeside with just a handful of laps to go to earn what proved to be a truly emotional victory.

The first of the races, held on Sunday afternoon, was the one held over from the rain-soaked opening round at Brands Hatch and it proved something of a benefit match for the Swan Yamaha team as Hill took the victory ahead of his team-mate Noriyuki Haga. It might have been a different story though, as Hill was only running in third place when the action was red-flagged because of Jon Kirkham's horrific high-speed crash at Druids where the Derby rider suffered concussion. Hill, however, was on the front row for the re-start, but did not get away too well and had to fight back into contention picking off Brookes, Haga and Byrne before taking his first win of the season.

The defending champion was in the hunt for more of the same in the final race of the weekend but Byrne had that little bit extra as he became the sixth different rider so far in the campaign to taste the victor's champagne. 'Shakey' celebrated but his Rapid Solicitors Kawasaki team was equally elated that Stuart Easton had chalked up his first podium finish of the campaign signalling that the former British Supersport champion was nearing a full recovery from injury.

Not so happy was Michael Laverty, one of the pre-season favourites for the crown, whose struggles with set-up and the subsequent grip issues was having a continuing struggle, although a test session immediately after this round was to solve them.

| BSB CHAMPIONSHIP POINTS | | |
|---|---|---|
| 1 | HILL | 98 |
| 2 | BROOKES | 92 |
| 3 | BYRNE | 88 |
| 4 | EASTON | 58 |
| 5 | LOWRY | 52 |
| 6 | SEELEY | 49 |

# *Race Bred, Race Blu*

Whatever the racing category, Yamaha are at the sharp end fighting for the silverware. The YZF-R1 with its cross-plane cranked, four cylinder, 16-valve, fuel injected engine and its smooth-as-silk traction control, is testament to the company's passion for motorcycle competition and is a graphic example of race track tech finding its way onto the road. And in our new Race Blu colours, it's looking great too.

Whether it's finance or Profile PCP, we have the deal to make the R1, or any other of our motorcycles and scooters, very affordable indeed. Be different, talk to one of our authorised Yamaha dealers now and strike while the deal is hot.

YZF-R6

# 04
# Snetterton
# 300
## 25 - 27 MAY 2012

**Above:** Josh Brookes and his girlfriend have to fight for the hair straighteners: Brookes loses!

**Top right:** The pack heads round turn one

**Bottom left:** Byrne and Brookes tough it out – Brookes taking away 12 points more than his rival

**Bottom right:** Tommy Hill leads Haga and Byrne

**Top left:** Michael Laverty had a better day on the Samsung Honda with a win and a second

**Far left:** Seeley had another dismal weekend and left Snetterton, pointless

**Top:** Lowry had a mediocre weekend, Easton not so good, and Haga ended with his head in the sand

**Left:** BSB's first lady, Jenny Tinmouth continued to learn her trade

**Above:** Tommy Hill stuffs his Swan Yamaha underneath Josh Brookes and (right) although Michael Rutter added plenty of rubber to the Norfolk circuit, he only added five points to his tally

# Snetterton 300

## LAVERTY BATTLES HIS WAY INTO CONTENTION…

Michael Laverty powered into the meeting knowing that he needed something special to put his title bid on course and the Ulsterman delivered the goods on a circuit where in pre-season testing he had packed the power and set the pace. The Samsung Honda rider chased down Tommy Hill in the opening race; losing out by little more than a second, but next time out he took his first victory of the season to signal his arrival in the title race.

But as Laverty smiled, Hill was frowning as he knew that overheating problems with his Swan Yamaha had cost him the chances of a double victory and also lost him the lead in the overall standings. Hill had experienced problems in the first race and believed they had been sorted. However, that was far from the case and he was sidelined early on in race two.

That left the way clear for Tyco Suzuki's Josh Brookes to nose ahead in the standings, though by only one solitary point as he rode consistently into a brace of third places. Brookes was enjoying his rides rather more than his team-mate Alastair Seeley who attracted national press attention for the wrong reasons as his bike bounced into the barrier at Richies during practice turning into a fireball as it bounced. Seeley was unscathed and the bike was re-built but two pointless rides ensued in the races.

The Rapid Solicitors Kawasaki duo of Shane Byrne and Stuart Easton also had machine problems in the opening race, Byrne jokingly referring to an 'electrical problem' as the team changed the engine in his bike ahead of the second race in which he repaid their efforts with a determined ride into second place.

There were many talking points across the weekend. Jon Kirkham making his racing comeback after his heavy tumble at Oulton Park not managing a lap in the opening race before crashing again under a harsh overtaking move by a rival. Noriyuki Haga showed the style and form expected in the opener, taking fourth ahead of Alex Lowes and Tommy Bridewell who by now had contracted to ride for Supersonic BMW for the full season, but the Japanese ace crashed out of race two which was to start an unfortunate pattern.

| BSB CHAMPIONSHIP POINTS | | |
|---|---|---|
| 1 | BROOKES | 124 |
| 2 | HILL | 123 |
| 3 | BYRNE | 108 |
| 4 | M LAVERTY | 81 |
| 5 | LOWRY | 73 |
| 6 | EASTON | 66 |

# MASERATI
## EXCELLENCE THROUGH PASSION

## PERFECT BALANCE

## THE NEW MASERATI GRANTURISMO SPORT

The new GranTurismo Sport features a number of subtle revisions to further enhance and improve the performance of this outstanding car. Available with either 6-speed, paddle-operated MC Shift manual or MC Shift Auto fully automatic transmission, the engine has been uprated to 460 horsepower. Suspension revisions improve the ride quality without affecting the superb handling balance. Inside the GranTurismo Sport features new front seats which not only improve comfort and support, but also allow for increased rear legroom. The GranTurismo Sport offers the optimum balance between performance and comfort and perfectly expresses Maserati's Grand Touring philosophy.

The Maserati GranTurismo Sport MC Shift Auto is priced at £90,750 on the road. The Maserati GranTurismo Sport MC Shift is priced at £94,080 on the road. On the road prices include 3 year/unlimited mileage warranty.

**For more information on the Maserati GranTurismo Sport or Maserati events please call 01943 871660.**

Car shown Maserati GranTurismo Sport MC Shift Auto with metallic paint at £564 and 20-inch Anthracite Grey Astro design alloy wheels at £480. Official fuel consumption for the Maserati GranTurismo Sport MC Shift Auto in mpg (litres/100 km): urban 12.9 (21.9), extra urban 28.8 (9.8), combined 19.7 (14.3). $CO_2$ emissions on combined cycle: 331 g/km.

# Knockhill

22 - 24 JUNE 2012

**Top:** Laverty and Byrne were racing hard

**Left:** Byrne was working the Rapid Solicitors Kawasaki hard over the start/finish (or maybe the Kawasaki was working Byrne hard?) whichever way, he left with a first and second place

**Above:** Dan Linfoot was trying hard on the Buildbase BMW while team-mate Barry Burrell took a tumble at the hairpin

**Top right:** Lowry was pushing hard chasing Brookes – a little too hard!

**Above:** Byrne runs up the inside of Hill at the hairpin while Swan Yamaha team mate 'Nitro' Nori Haga bombed again and crashed out

**Right:** Hill chases Byrne over the kerbs while Laverty kept Hill honest at the hairpin

**Right:** The 'Wee Wizard', Alastair Seeley was looking smooth but lacked the pace to make it count

**Below:** Tom Tunstall was back on his trusty Honda but still struggled while the Championship top four raced hard at the front

**Bottom right:** Tommy Hill managed to put some tarmac between himself and Josh Brookes in race two

# Knockhill

## BYRNE AND LAVERTY SHARE SCOTTISH SPOILS

Shane Byrne aboard the Rapid Solicitors Kawasaki firmly underlined his determination to take the domestic crown for a third time with a victory and a second place but in a series that by then had seen seven different riders taking the victories he knew that nothing would come easily.

This point was reinforced in the second race as Michael Laverty powered to his second win in three races to consolidate his all important place among the top six as he focussed on a place in the end of term 'Showdown' title decider.

For Samsung Honda rider Laverty the victory was all the sweeter as it eloquently answered the comments by one of his rivals that the win at Snetterton was simply a one-off because of the amount of pre-season testing he had done there. His points haul in Scotland was all the richer with a third place, adrift of Tommy Hill and Byrne in the opener.

Hill racked up points and podium credits, placing second and third on the Swan Yamaha, and but for a brake problem in the second race felt he could have done better. Even so, he moved back on top of the standings ahead of Byrne as Tyco Suzuki's Josh Brookes, twice placed fourth, dropped back to third place.

Tommy Bridewell, clearly enjoying his time with Supersonic BMW, continued his consistent form, running fifth and sixth and that booked the Wiltshire rider a place in the top six just a couple of points down on Ian Lowry who was having another troubled time. The Padgetts Honda rider had been running in the top five in both races but he tipped off at Scotsman in the opener and then had rear grip issues in the second which left him running back in tenth place.

Bravest performance of the round was provided by the gutsy Chris Walker. He had crashed his Pr1mo Bournemouth Kawasaki heavily in first free practice suffering a pair of broken heels. He shrugged aside the pain to qualify on the sixth row but in both races had to pull off with machine issues.

Missing his home round was Stuart Easton. He watched the action on TV from his Hawick home as he recovered from surgery to both clear up an infection and remove the fixator from the hip broken in his North West 200 crash. His absence cost him his place in the top six.

| BSB CHAMPIONSHIP POINTS | | |
|---|---|---|
| 1 | HILL | 159 |
| 2 | BYRNE | 153 |
| 3 | BROOKES | 150 |
| 4 | M LAVERTY | 122 |
| 5 | LOWRY | 79 |
| 6 | BRIDEWELL | 77 |

# Nearly all men can stand adversity, but if you want to test a man's character, give him power!

Abraham Lincoln

# 06
# Oulton Park

06 - 08 JULY 2012

**Left:** Byrne pushes Laverty hard but **below:** Tommy Hill was on fire and took all three race wins of the weekend and with it, the lead in the Championship race and valuable podium credits

**Right:** PBM's regular Superstock rider, Keith Farmer deputised for Stuart Easton as he was side-lined and was given a demonstration lap by the maestro, 'Shakey' Byrne

**Bottom right:** Tyco Suzuki's Josh Brookes was pushing and he, Hill and Byrne were the only three riders to step on the podium all weekend

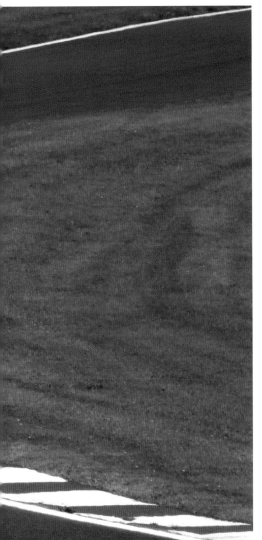

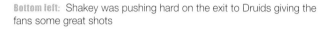

**Bottom left:** Shakey was pushing hard on the exit to Druids giving the fans some great shots

**Centre:** Shane Byrne with Olympic medallist Beth Tweddle

**Below:** Keith Farmer acquitted himself well on the PBM Kawasaki but his focus was on victory in the Superstock class and he failed to score points in the races

**Top left:** Try as he might, Jon Kirkam struggled to get to grips at the circuit where he had a massive crash at the first visit in May and left adding just two points to his tally

**Top right:** Scott Smart managed to add a few points to his total

**Left:** Tommy Hill dives into the lead at turn one

**Above:** Alastair Seeley interviewed by Eurosport's resident expert former British and World Championship racer, James Whitham

**Right:** Lincolnshire lad Peter Hickman turns on the style on his Buildbase BMW

# Oulton Park

## TOMMY AT THE TREBLE!

Tommy Hill was both imperious and a rider in a hurry as he dominated this triple race round at the Cheshire circuit. The Swan Yamaha man had powered to pole for the opening race and then underlined his domination by being headed for less than a quarter of a mile across the three races, such was his style and speed.

The reigning champion left the pretenders to his crown in no doubt that they have a fight on their hands if they are to get ahead of him, but Hill barely had time to celebrate his first hat-trick in the series as he took his win tally to five in the current series, before he was jetting off to Japan for a test ahead of the Suzuka Eight Hours race.

Hill was leading Saturday's race with the rejuvenated Michael Laverty running a close second in the early stages only for the Samsung Honda rider to crash out at Britten's forcing Shane Byrne and Josh Brookes, who were running in close formation, to take avoiding action, before continuing a vain pursuit. Brookes took second for Tyco Suzuki, almost five seconds down on Hill whilst Byrne was third ahead of Noriyuki Haga.

Sunday's first race saw Hill make the break initially followed by Haga though the Japanese rider was soon swallowed up by the hard riding Brookes who was again destined to be second, this time by three seconds with Rapid Solicitors Kawasaki's Byrne third from Laverty.

Brookes became the first and only rider to nose ahead of Hill when he briefly grabbed the lead on the second lap before normal service was resumed and, as the scrap for positions behind Hill intensified. Laverty, Haga, Byrne and Brookes were hungry to end the weekend on a high but Byrne it was who came through in second from Brookes with Haga, Laverty and Alex Lowes, all of whom had ridden well and Lowes posing questions of the others on the WFR Honda.

The fight to secure placings among the elite six who will go forward to the Showdown sequence heated up and the alarm bells were ringing for a number of riders, among them Ian Lowry, who was counting the cost of a first race tumble as he slipped to seventh overall and Chris Walker who was unable to repeat his earlier heroics at the circuit. Jon Kirkham, needing strong results to make up ground lost by his tumble at Oulton in May, had a troubled weekend and Stuart Easton missed out for a second time through injury.

| BSB CHAMPIONSHIP POINTS | | |
|---|---|---|
| 1 | HILL | 234 |
| 2 | BROOKES | 206 |
| 3 | BYRNE | 205 |
| 4 | M LAVERTY | 146 |
| 5 | BRIDEWELL | 104 |
| 6 | HAGA | 102 |

# RUNAROUND OR THRILLER

Choose from a range of bike loans to suit you, available from your local dealer.

Contact your local dealer or visit
**blackhorse.co.uk**

# Brands Hatch GP

**20 - 22 JULY 2012**

**Top:** Laverty pushed on but was hampered by technical issues

**Top right:** A huge crowd basked in the Brands Hatch sunshine for the start of the Superbike races

**Bottom right:** It's standing room only as a packed grandstand watch the drama unfold at Paddock Hill Bend

**Top left:** 'The Rocker", Luca Scassa – stylish as usual

**Bottom left:** Shane "Shakey" Byrne winds it up as he passes the impressive hospitality of the Motorsportvision Centre out of Clearways and on to the start /finish straight

**Left:** Despite his obvious talent, Michael "Blade" Rutter had a disappointing weekend

**Above:** There was an 'eye-watering' incident at the bottom of Paddock Hill bend for Westmoreland as he ran off track

**Left:** Alex Lowes obviously has immense potential and although he didn't finish with the 'big boys' he was progressing in the right direction

**Above:** Laverty and Hill discuss their race for third and fourth places respectively

**Right:** Byrne gives team-mate Easton a lift back to the pits at the end of race two

**Below:** The class of the field was starting to show as Byrne leads Laverty, Hill and Brookes out of Surtees on his way to a daily double of race wins

# Brands Hatch GP

## SHAKEY RULES AT HOME TRACK

Shane 'Shakey' Byrne ruled supreme as he powered in a winning double at his home circuit taking his score so far to four victories. The Rapid Solicitors Kawasaki rider finished each race ahead of Josh Brookes and Tommy Hill and those points hauls ensured that all three of them had a guaranteed place among the six 'Title Fighters' going into the Showdown.

Byrne, who moved into second place in the overall standings behind Hill, was quick to praise the hard work of his team who had ironed out the gremlins that had slowed him in the previous round, giving his bike the added drive it was lacking out of the corners. That, as well as his own work on personal fitness, paid handsome dividends and Byrne showed that by scorching to pole.

But in each race it was Michael Laverty who forged into the early albeit short-lived lead aboard his Samsung Honda before Byrne asserted himself and took control. Hill experienced clutch problems on his Swan Yamaha at the start and had to make adjustments as the race progressed as his team-mate Noriyuki Haga settled into his rhythm to run second before being taken by the determined Tyco Suzuki riding Brookes.

Haga looked set for a podium finish but amid an inconsistent term the Japanese rider fell at Graham Hill Bend handing third to Hill as Laverty ran fourth ahead of Supersonic BMW's Tommy Bridewell, again riding strongly and looking at ease at the sharp end of the pack.

Byrne was leading by the end of the opening lap of the second encounter on the Grand Prix circuit and as hard as Brookes tried there was no way through for the Aussie who in turn was clear of Hill. Behind them, the squabble for points to earn a Showdown spot was intensifying. Laverty eased within reach as he completed a brace of fourths ahead of Haga with whom he had scrapped for much of the race.

Alex Lowes maintained his challenge with a sixth place on the WFR Honda, just ahead of Bridewell while Ian Lowry made up some ground lost by his first race tumble from the Padgetts Honda as he took seventh in the race. Chris Walker and Stuart Easton also suffered costly tumbles to leave them under pressure but not as much as that experienced by first round winner Jon Kirkham who just scraped into the points in mid-pack.

| BSB CHAMPIONSHIP POINTS | | |
|---|---|---|
| 1 | HILL | 266 |
| 2 | BYRNE | 255 |
| 3 | BROOKES | 246 |
| 4 | M LAVERTY | 172 |
| 5 | BRIDEWELL | 124 |
| 6 | HAGA | 113 |

# job done.

**SHOEI**®
## PREMIUM HELMETS

discover why 'Shakey' chooses Shoei at **www.shoeiassured.co.uk**

shoeihelmets.uk

# 08
# Cadwell Park
**25 - 27 AUGUST 2012**

**Above:** Tommy Hill likes Cadwell Park – the scene of his first BSB victory. Here he heads Laverty and the rest of the pack on his way to a double victory

**Right:** Brookes takes a lonely line through Hall Bends and his weekend didn't quite deliver the results he would have liked (and indeed needed)

**Below:** The GBmoto Hondas of Tristan Palmer and Luke Quigley didn't take any points for Lincolnshire, but they were well turned out as usual

**Bottom right:** James Westmoreland is chased hard by Ian Lowry on his way to a couple of good results

**Top left:** Tommy Bridewell had been scoring regularly all season and was consistent again at Cadwell Park

**Left:** Michael Laverty started to get some good feeling back with his Honda and took two strong podium results away at his Samsung Honda team's local circuit

**Above:** With his team-mate out due to a shoulder injury, it was left to Stuart Easton to fly the PBM flag, but still recovering from his earlier ailments he struggled and left with only two points for his efforts

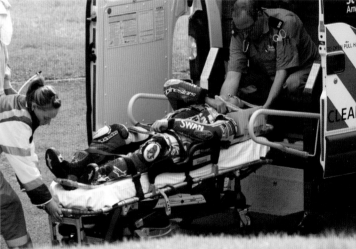

# 08 Cadwell Park

## CRASH AND BYRNE...

After a five week break, Tommy Hill dictated terms with an emphatic winning double aboard his Swan Yamaha, taking his victory tally for the season to seven and while the reigning champion was already assured of his place among the six title fighters, these results accrued another six podium credit scores that could be so crucial in the final outcome of the crown.

If Hill was thrilled, then so too was Lincolnshire lad Alex Lowes, who finally realised his potential on a circuit where he and his twin brother Sam had cut their racing teeth. Riding the WFR Honda, Lowes powered in his second career pole start, and the first for the team, then rode to second place in the opening race to claim his and the team's first podium finish. That was followed up by a determined ride into fourth place in race two, and Lowes was in the top six.

Josh Brookes, like Hill already confirmed for the Showdown, had struggled in qualifying, starting from the fourth row, but, with his crowd pleasing leaps high over the Mountain crest, the Aussie brought his Tyco Suzuki into second place in race two after a sixth place in the opener.

In each of the races Samsung Honda's Michael Laverty, having made the early break to lead, had to settle for a pair of third placings. It did, however, seal his place in the Showdown and gave him a couple of podium credits whilst the other rider already qualified, the former two times title winner Shane Byrne, could only watch the action and in some discomfort at that.

Byrne had crashed heavily and awkwardly from his Rapid Solicitors Kawasaki at Hall Bends in Saturday free practice sustaining complex ligament damage. He underwent surgery in Manchester the following day and returned to the circuit on Monday but was unable to ride.

And there was another fall-guy when Noriyuki Haga tipped off his Swan Yamaha at Mansfield breaking a collarbone which ruled him out of the races and as a result dropped him out of the all important top six as he was overtaken not only by Lowes, but also Ian Lowry with James Westmoreland in close contention.

The revelation of the meeting was young Danny Buchan, racing in BSB for only the second time, but bringing his MSS Bathams Kawasaki home in fourth place in the opener. It was a pity he tumbled early on in race two but Buchan established himself as one to watch in the future.

| BSB CHAMPIONSHIP POINTS | | |
|---|---|---|
| 1 | HILL | 316 |
| 2 | BROOKES | 276 |
| 3 | BYRNE | 255 |
| 4 | M LAVERTY | 204 |
| 5 | BRIDEWELL | 142 |
| 6 | LOWES | 126 |

# Thank you for a great season

To all of our co-sponsors, team members and customers a huge thank you for what was a fantatstic season in 2012 and looking forward to 2013.

For more information:
Email: info@tyco-suzuki.co.uk
Visit: www.tyco-suzuki.co.uk

**tyco**
Security Products

# 09

# Donington Park

07 - 09 September 2012

**Left:** The pack thunders through Redgate on lap one

**Right:** Poor old Alastair Seeley had more bad fortune and Michael Rutter was certainly not running where he wanted to be (bottom left)

**Below:** Stuart Easton was getting back to form and finished with a couple of solid points scoring rides, but with him missing a couple of earlier rounds, it was not enough to see him join the 'Title Fighters' for the Showdown

**Top:** Alex Lowes did enough to secure his place in the Showdown and with it an outside chance of taking the crown

**Left and below:** Josh Brookes was unbeatable as he took his first BSB double of the season at Donington

**Right:** Although Danny Buchan had been looking good on the MSS Kawasaki, he failed to convert that form into points

**Above:** Scott Smart took a tumble

Peter Hickman added just two points to his tally while Josh Brookes added fifty and valuable podium credits going into the Showdown [right]

# Donington Park

## BROOKES AT THE DOUBLE

Josh Brookes was the dominant force across the whole weekend which saw him take pole position before setting the fastest laps in each of the two races as he took his first ever double BSB victory.

It was his first winning rides since he had last tasted the victor's champagne back in April at Thruxton and it was a clear signal of intent that the Aussie and Tyco Suzuki were ready and raring to go in the Showdown sequence that followed on from this round and it set a benchmark for the rest. Brookes had gone into the Leicestershire circuit already qualified as a Title Fighter, together with Tommy Hill, Michael Laverty and Shane Byrne who wisely decided not to race to avoid any further injury to his right shoulder.

It was the crucial round for the rest who were aiming for the final two places among the elite six and there were eight riders in with a chance. Amongst them was Noriyuki Haga, paying the cost of a hugely inconsistent season, who had to shrug aside the pain of his broken collarbone in a vain attempt to make the cut aboard his Swan Yamaha. It was too much of an ask as the Japanese ace scored only a handful of points and Ian Lowry was also out of the equation as he fell from his Padgetts Honda in the opening race.

Taking full advantage was Alex Lowes who continued the blistering pace he had shown in the previous round aboard the WFR Honda to secure a front row start and then translating that into sixth and fifth place finishes. The results saw Lowes through where he joined the determined Tommy Bridewell who had scored points in every round bar one aboard the Supersonic Racing BMW. Bridewell, who didn't have a ride on the eve of the season, had clinched his place in race one and with the shackles of qualification off, he romped to his and BMW's best result of the season of fourth in race two.

The best of the rest was James Westmoreland, but for him, along with Haga, Lowry, Chris Walker, Stuart Easton and Alastair Seeley the focus turned to the BSB Riders Cup as they rued missed opportunities across the first 19 races.

| BSB CHAMPIONSHIP POINTS | | |
|---|---|---|
| 1 | HILL | 352 |
| 2 | BROOKES | 326 |
| 3 | BYRNE | 255 |
| 4 | M LAVERTY | 240 |
| 5 | BRIDEWELL | 162 |
| 6 | LOWES | 146 |

| BSB SHOWDOWN STANDINGS | | |
|---|---|---|
| 1 | HILL | 535 |
| 2 | BROOKES | 525 |
| 3 | BYRNE | 523 |
| 4 | M LAVERTY | 514 |
| 5 | LOWES | 502 |
| 6 | BRIDEWELL | 500 |

# 10

## THE SHOWDOWN

# TT Circuit Assen

### 21 - 23 September 2012

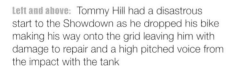

**Left and above:** Tommy Hill had a disastrous start to the Showdown as he dropped his bike making his way onto the grid leaving him with damage to repair and a high pitched voice from the impact with the tank

**Right:** Jon Kirkham was still struggling to regain his early season form while Tommy Bridewell who had somewhat crept into the Showdown under the radar had a couple of solid finishes

**Below:** Shakey heads the pack at the end of the long start straight at Assen

**Above:** Brookes riding the only way he knows how - aggressive and on the edge - or in this case, just over it

**Bottom right:** Michael Laverty made a couple of strong starts but faded as his handling problems returned to haunt him

**Bottom left and top right:** Shakey went on to take a win and a second place as he and Brookes shared the spoils

# TT Circuit Assen

## BROOKES AND BYRNE GO DUTCH...

The historic first ever round of BSB on mainland Europe provided its own blend of drama and thrills as the Showdown began at Assen with varying fortunes for the elite six riders who had earned their Title Fighter status as they raced in front of a bumper 30,000 crowd.

Qualifying had been straightforward enough as the riders clearly enjoyed the challenges of riding the fast, flowing Dutch circuit and it was Alex Lowes who continued his timely late season rich vein of form as he powered to his second pole start in three rounds aboard the WFR Honda to signal to everyone, if they needed convincing, that far from making up the numbers in the final title deciding sequence, he was a real challenger.

For Tommy Hill the drama began even before the first race had started. He arrived at the starting grid, busy with mechanics tending their riders' machines, but as he rode through to his position, someone clipped his Swan Yamaha, jamming on the front brake and throwing him over the bars. Hill was OK but the bike was damaged and the vastly experienced Yamaha team made a hasty repair enabling a pit-lane start to earn a time and decent grid position for race two.

The race got underway and saw Michael Laverty make the break on his Samsung Honda, though he was soon taken by Shane Byrne aboard the Rapid Solicitors Kawasaki. Laverty regained the advantage briefly but, slowing with tyre issues, he dropped back to an eventual seventh. Byrne took charge, taking his fifth victory of the season comfortably clear of Tyco Suzuki's Josh Brookes who had penned a year-long extension to his contract with the team prior to the meeting. Lowes came through in third but Hill was left frustrated, watching from the pits having pulled in after six laps.

Next time out and again it was an early Laverty v Byrne confrontation, but soon Byrne was in charge. However Brookes, riding superbly, was on the charge, coming through from fifth in the early stages to take the lead with three laps remaining. Byrne nosed back in front going into the final lap but, as he struggled to hold his line through the last left-hander before the chicane due to his shoulder injury not being back to full strength, Brookes timed his move perfectly to grab the lead and win the dash to the line by a quarter of a second and take the lead in the standings. Lowes also left it late, muscling his way past Hill to take third place.

Laverty was again struggling after his early promise, finishing seventh again, just adrift of the Title Fighter Tommy Bridewell aboard the Supersonic BMW who followed up his fifth place in race one with a sixth in race two.

| BSB CHAMPIONSHIP POINTS | | |
|---|---|---|
| 1 | BROOKES | 570 |
| 2 | BYRNE | 568 |
| 3 | HILL | 548 |
| 4 | LOWES | 534 |
| 5 | M LAVERTY | 532 |
| 6 | BRIDEWELL | 521 |

# Silverstone
# Arena GP

**28 - 30 SEPTEMBER 2012**

11

THE SHOWDOWN

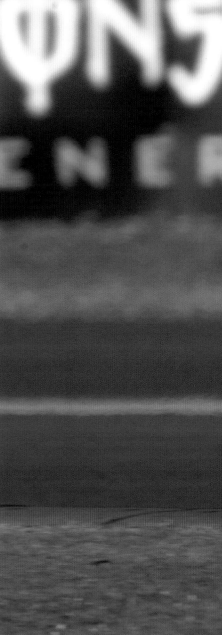

Above: Tommy Hill struggled at Silverstone and although Shakey was on form (right) he had to take second place in each race behind a hungry Alex Lowes

Bottom right: Laverty appeared to be getting his feeling back and rode to a couple of strong finishes

**Left:** Jacub Smrz joined in the Showdown fun on the Splitlath Redmond Aprilia and soon learned how hot the pace in BSB is

**Above:** Alex Lowes was 'onit' and had an unforgettable weekend as he nicked the race wins from Byrne to give himself and the WFR team their maiden double victory

**Left:** Patric Muff struggled while team-mate Bridewell remained consistent **(below)**

**Right:** Brookes took a third and a fourth on the day but that was not enough to prevent Shakey taking the Championship lead

**Below:** Alex Lowes celebrates his Team's first double victory

**Right:** Seeley and Haga both struggled at the Northamptonshire circuit

# Silverstone Arena GP

## LOWES STUNS SILVERSTONE...

Alex Lowes blew the title chase wide open as he followed up his third pole start in four rounds by powering his WFR Honda to a stunning maiden race winning double at Silverstone's Arena GP track.

The Lincolnshire lad had left it late to show his potential, but these performances left no-one in doubt that both he and his highly professional team would be the ones to watch.

Lowes made light of the issues of tyre wear, lack of grip and the chilly conditions as others struggled, most noticeably the reigning champion Tommy Hill who gambled wrongly on the tyre choice for his Swan Yamaha in the opening race and ended the day with a pair of sevenths that dropped him to fourth in the rankings.

Also struggling was Michael Laverty who worked frantically with his Samsung Honda team to find a compromise setting that would give him the chance to peg back points and while he managed a podium finish in the opener, he struggled into fifth next time out and like Hill was seeing his hopes of taking the silverware diminishing.

Silverstone, with its long, fast configuration, posed the questions for everyone and former two times title winner Shane Byrne was an early casualty, crashing in free practice and severely damaging his Rapid Solicitors Kawasaki but lengthy overnight work saw him back on track, only for another major technical problem on Sunday morning to prevent him going out in the warm-up practice. Byrne, the master craftsman, was able to ride his way around that while Josh Brookes, riding the Tyco Suzuki, also had to overcome riding with a tyre compound which, while not his preferred choice, he made work.

The races were absolute crackers. Laverty led the opener but Lowes swooped into the lead at Stowe on the third lap. Byrne challenged and briefly snatched the lead but straight-lined a corner and lost ground but fought back. Tommy Bridewell showed in flashes why he had made Title Fighter status running second for several laps on the Supersonic BMW. Lowes led from Laverty but in the closing stages Byrne took second from the Ulsterman with Brookes fourth.

Next time out Byrne and Laverty duelled for the lead, trading places to half distance before Lowes took over at the front for a couple of laps. Byrne regained the advantage and going into Woodcote for the final time looked set for a sixth win of the season, but Lowes had other ideas, pulling off a move that was audacious and in his own words 'cheeky' to grab the win by half a machine's length. Byrne was second ahead of Brookes, Bridewell and Laverty.

| BSB CHAMPIONSHIP POINTS | | |
|---|---|---|
| 1 | BYRNE | 608 |
| 2 | BROOKES | 599 |
| 3 | LOWES | 584 |
| 4 | HILL | 566 |
| 5 | M LAVERTY | 559 |
| 6 | BRIDEWELL | 544 |

# Brands Hatch GP

**12-14 OCTOBER 2012**

12

THE SHOWDOWN

**Left:** It's all go as the Championship finale gets under way

**Above:** Byrne was in a class of his own all weekend at his favourite circuit

**Bottom left:** Brookes was looking tired and rough as the strains of the season took their toll

**Below:** Everyone fights for the same strip of tarmac into Druids on lap one

**Top left:** Alex Lowes was pushing hard until a crash at the damp Clearways ended his title hopes

**Top right:** Brookes put his heart and soul into the racing and pushed Byrne all the way but with Byrne on top form he was unable to do enough

**Above:** The calm before the storm

**Right:** Barry Burrell put his strongest performance of the season together and was mixing it with the leaders (far right)

**Left:** Michael Rutter didn't have the best end of season results on his Bathams backed MSS Kawasaki but aims to be back for another shot in 2013

**Right:** Once again, the sun shone on the massive Brands Hatch crowd

**Bottom right:** Brookes pushed hard and even into the final race of the season was in with a chance of the crown

**Top left:** James Westmoreland had a good outing on the WFR Honda ending the season in seventh place overall and taking the Riders' Cup

**Above:** Alex Lowes crashes out of second place as the light drizzle suddenly became heavier and is consoled by Byrne as he walks back to the paddock (left)

**Below left:** Barry Burrell made good progress and dices with Michael Laverty

**Below:** Alex Lowes is chased down by Michael Laverty - the pair eventually ended up in the gravel at Paddock Hill after an ambitious last lap move by Lowes

# Brands Hatch GP

## BYRNE WRAPS IT UP IN STYLE...

Alex Lowes was ready to take the fight to Shane Byrne and Josh Brookes and he showed that determination as he scorched the WFR Honda to a fourth pole start in five rounds but this time the Lincolnshire lad was unable to capitalise on it amid a weekend of bitter disappointment.

He was an unwitting victim of the light rain that shortened the first of the three decisive races as once again the Showdown provided a nail-biting finale packed with drama and excitement. The master of it all was Shane Byrne who ruled imperiously to take the crown for a record equalling third time as he completed a brilliant hat-trick of race wins.

Having worked tirelessly with his Rapid Solicitors Kawasaki team across free practice to ensure his bike was in top condition and set up perfectly for race distances, it was Byrne who grabbed the initiative in the Saturday afternoon curtain raiser. He took the lead and was never headed as behind him Lowes and Samsung Honda's Michael Laverty squabbled for second before the Ulsterman was forced wide in one of many attempted overtaking moves.

Tommy Hill gained most, coming through into third place ahead of Josh Brookes, but going into the final third of the race, light rain was reported in several areas and the red flags came out as race leader Byrne completed his 15th lap. The race stoppage came seconds too late for Lowes who slid off at the greasy Clearways whilst Swan Yamaha's Hill had second from Brookes.

Byrne had worked out his sums and knew what he had to do going into Sunday's first race but then he was confused by his pit signals. It took him some time to realise that it was Buildbase BMW's Barry Burrell heading the battle behind him in a race punctuated by two safety car interventions resulting in a three-lap extension to the distance. Byrne powered on, taking his seventh victory of the season as Brookes brought his Tyco Suzuki into second place ahead of Laverty.

All this meant Byrne needed two points in the final race of the season to seal the crown while Brookes needed to win and his rival to be sidelined. The Aussie did everything that he could, taking the lead for much of the race, but Byrne was always in close contention and then on the penultimate lap he pulled off an audacious move at Pilgrims Drop to charge ahead of Brookes. It was a risk, but one well taken by Byrne who wanted nothing less than a winning ride to clinch his title and with his eighth win, he did that in style.

But the drama continued to the end. Lowes, eager to show what might have been after a first machine failure of the season had ruled him out of the penultimate race, was duelling with Laverty for third on the last lap going into Paddock Hill Bend, but they both went down leaving the outgoing champion Hill to take third.

| BSB CHAMPIONSHIP STANDINGS | | |
|---|---|---|
| 1 | BYRNE | 683 |
| 2 | BROOKES | 655 |
| 3 | HILL | 612 |
| 4 | LOWES | 584 |
| 5 | M LAVERTY | 581 |
| 6 | BRIDEWELL | 577 |

# Motorpoint British Supersport Championship
## Protected by Datatag

## RICHARDS TRIUMPHS AGAIN!

Having been treated to a thrilling British Supersport Championship in 2011, few would have expected 2012 to have come anywhere near in terms of entertainment and drama. But it did just that and, if anything, surpassed it as Australian Glen Richards took the crown from Jack Kennedy at the final round.

Practically every race saw at least six riders fighting it out for the race wins and whilst Richards and Kennedy took 13 wins between them, they were made to fight hard by the likes of Billy McConnell, Christian Iddon, Ben Wilson, Richard Cooper, Sam Warren, Luke Mossey and Pauli Pekkanen.

Kennedy stole the early advantage on his Mar-Train Yamaha as Richards gradually got into his stride on the Smiths Racing Triumph but it was in the final third of the season that the pendulum swung most. When Richards crashed at Donington, on a discarded tear-off visor of all things, it appeared to hand the advantage back to Dubliner Kennedy but he then suffered a succession of front end crashes at Assen and Silverstone which meant Richards led by 12.5pts going into the final round.

The two races at the Kent venue were nothing short of sensational. With one lap to go of the first race, Richards was leading with Kennedy back in fourth which would have all but given the 2008 champion another title with just one race to go but with no team orders, Richards' team-mate McConnell had other ideas and went all out for the win which he duly took. In the final lap sort out, Kennedy took second with Richards in third bringing the gap back to 8.5pts.

Richards then made a mistake when he missed a gear and crashed in the final race, seemingly handing the title to Kennedy who then suffered his first mechanical DNF of the year and retired meaning 39-year-old Richards was champion in the most surreal of fashions. McConnell, who ended the year with six wins, was no doubt the most relieved man of the paddock and finished in third overall, only a couple of low scores at Assen preventing him from being in title contention at the final round.

Iddon and Cooper got stronger as the year wore on with their Oxford TAG Triumphs always in the thick of the action, the former particularly impressive as he strung together a strong second half of the season including two wins. Cooper, the 2011 Superstock 1000 champion was a lot slower out of the blocks but eventually proved his worth whilst Wilson, although not as strong as 2011, was always there or thereabouts. Warren, meanwhile, was the early season pace setter until he suffered a number of crashes and eventually split with the Seton Tuning Yamaha team.

The battle for the Motorpoint Supersport Cup was disputed between youngsters Glenn Irwin and Luke Jones and such was their pace, they were regularly finishing the races in the top eight overall. Jones had the honour of being the first Cup rider to stand on a championship podium but Irwin just had the edge and ended the year as the deserved champion.

| CHAMPIONSHIP POSITIONS | | | |
|---|---|---|---|
| 1 | Glen RICHARDS | *(Triumph)* | **372** |
| 2 | Jack KENNEDY | *(Yamaha)* | **363.5** |
| 3 | Billy McCONNELL | *(Triumph)* | **340** |
| 4 | Christian IDDON | *(Triumph)* | **285.5** |
| 5 | Ben Wilson | *(Kawasaki)* | **259** |
| 6 | Richard Cooper | *(Triumph)* | **221** |

## FARMER DOES IT AGAIN

Having dominated the National Superstock 600 Championship in 2011, Keith Farmer stepped up to the 1000cc class in 2012 and promptly took title number two on the Rapid Solicitors Kawasaki in just his second full season of road racing.

The 25-year-old Ulsterman ran under the wing of the Paul Bird Motorsport team and started with a bang by taking the first two rounds of the season, one in the wet and one in the dry, to prove he was the man for all seasons. He then suffered a slight dip in form but it was only brief and he only finished off the podium once in the last seven races, ending the year with five wins and eight podiums to his name.

It was Jason O'Halloran on the Samsung Honda that pushed him hardest, the Australian rider returning strongly after suffering serious injury the previous year. A brace of podiums at the beginning of the season set up his title challenge and with three wins in six races, he was right on Farmer's tail. However, a broken gear lever at the penultimate round saw his hopes disappear and he had to settle for second overall.

Aside from Farmer, Jimmy Storrar (JS Racing BMW) and Danny Buchan set the early pace, the former putting together a string of runner-up spots in the first half of the season and the latter taking a race win and podiums once he'd switched back to the MSS Kawasaki team from CN Racing who he'd started the year with. Storrar's challenge faded away whilst Buchan eventually moved up to BSB. That meant it was Victor Cox who came through the pack to take third overall, the ILR Kawasaki rider taking three podiums along the way as he became the only rider to score points at every round.

The action was again fast and furious at each round and the BMW trio of David Johnson, Steve Brogan and Howie Mainwaring were always at the forefront, Australian rider Johnson often the quickest in qualifying but also out of luck in the races. He did claim a debut win at Oulton Park in July but, amazingly, failed to finish a race after that whilst Buildbase team-mates Brogan and Mainwaring both starred at various times of the year.

Lee Costello was undoubtedly the most improved rider of the year and, having only managed 14 points in 2011, he added 100 to that tally in 2012 with his second half of the year being particularly impressive as he took the race win at Silverstone.

Adam Jenkinson, Jonathan Railton, Daniel Johnson, Joe Burns, Patrick Medcalf, Lee Johnston and John McGuinness were other riders to feature prominently during the year but the biggest impression of all was made by American PJ Jacobsen. Riding the Tyco Suzuki, initially for one round only, the 21 year old went on to win at Donington Park and take two further podiums to put him right in contention for a BSB ride in 2013.

| CHAMPIONSHIP POSITIONS | | |
|---|---|---|
| 1 | Keith FARMER *(Kawasaki)* | 207 |
| 2 | Jason O'HALLORAN *(Honda)* | 157 |
| 3 | Victor COX *(Kawasaki)* | 142 |
| 4 | Jimmy STORRAR *(BMW)* | 117 |
| 5 | Lee COSTELLO *(Kawasaki)* | 114 |
| 6 | Howie MAINWARING *(BMW)* | 105 |

# Metzeler National Superstock 600 Championship

## JACKSON EXCELS ON FOUR-STROKE DEBUT

A steady start to the season gave little indication about what lay ahead for Lee Jackson in the Metzeler National Superstock 600 Championship but once the former 125cc front-runner got his first podium at the WSB meeting at Donington Park in May, he never looked back.

Benefitting from the tutelage of Chris Walker, the 16-year-old simply got quicker as the year progressed and as he got more used to the four-stroke, so his championship challenge snowballed. Four wins in the last six rounds was ultimately what propelled Jackson to title glory but he still had to wait until the final round to wrap it all up.

Australian rider Ben Burke (Seton Tuning Yamaha) went into the final race level on points with Jackson, his title effort peaking mid season when a run of three straight wins looked like it would see him get the better of his rivals but his dream faded at the end of the year when a crash at Silverstone and a retirement at Brands Hatch saw him fail to score a point when it mattered most.

James Rose also had a chance of claiming the championship at the final round, despite the Moto Breakers Yamaha rider failing to win a race all year. Consistent top six finishes, including six podiums, kept him in contention but he was taken out at the first corner at Brands Hatch and he ended the year in third just ahead of rapid team-mate Jake Dixon.

Son of former World Sidecar champion Darren, Dixon came out of the blocks the quickest with a win and three podiums from the first four races but his inexperience showed and five DNFs was ultimately what kept him in fourth. Nevertheless, he took three wins over the course of the season and will certainly come back stronger in 2013.

As always, it was consistency that paid dividends but there were also star performances during the year from Alex Olsen (Haribo Triumph), Josh Wainwright (AP Kawasaki), James Lodge (Moto Breakers Yamaha) and Johnny Blackshaw (Smiths Triumph) with Olsen claiming a race win at Donington Park. Grant Whitaker and Tim Hastings were also victorious but experienced up and down campaigns which was enough to keep them down in ninth and 11th respectively overall.

| | CHAMPIONSHIP POSITIONS | |
|---|---|---|
| 1 | Lee JACKSON *(Kawasaki)* | 199 |
| 2 | Ben BURKE *(Yamaha)* | 174 |
| 3 | James ROSE *(Yamaha)* | 169 |
| 4 | Jake DIXON *(Yamaha)* | 135 |
| 5 | Alex OLSEN *(Triumph)* | 105 |
| 6 | Josh WAINWRIGHT *(Kawasaki)* | 98 |

## LUKE HEDGES HIS BETS...

When it comes down to winning championships, it's all about being the most consistent rider over the course of the season and in the inaugural Monster Energy Motostar Championship, Luke Hedger was exactly that.

The FPW Racing rider only failed to finish one race all year and out of the other eleven, he was never out of the top six so that, along with two wins and six podiums enabled him to wrap up the crown with a round to spare. His eventual winning margin was a commanding 60 points and having finished fourth in 2011, he certainly stepped up to the plate in 2012.

His main rivals during the season split their time between the British Championship and the Red Bull Rookies Cup so missed a few of the rounds but when they attended, Bradley Ray, Kyle Ryde, Jordan Weaving and Tarran Mackenzie were always battling it out for the race wins.

Ray (SP125/FAB Racing Honda) was the quickest of the quartet and won all five of the races he finished to end the year in second overall with Ryde, on one of the few Moto3 machines on the grid, taking three victories. Weaving, on another of the Steve Patrickson-fettled Hondas, finished on the podium in five of the six races he completed whilst Mackenzie, youngest son of former GP rider Niall, rode the only KTM in the field to stand on the rostrum on two occasions.

There were only two other winners during the season but one of those was a history making victor as Catherine Green (RS Racing Honda) became the first female ever to win a British Championship race when she dominated proceedings at Cadwell Park. Had it not been for a slow start to the season, when she only scored 20 points in the first four rounds, she could well have challenged Hedger further but third overall in the title table was still an excellent achievement.

Harry Stafford took the race win at Silverstone, his only appearance in the series all season, and so it was left to the likes of Joe Irving, Joe Francis, Tom Carne, Philip Wakefield and Ryan Watson to challenge for the leaderboard placings week in week out. Hedger also got the verdict in the Motostar Cup, again by 60 points, with Francis, Irving, Ray, Ryde and Weaving completing the top six.

### CHAMPIONSHIP POSITIONS

| | | |
|---|---|---|
| 1 | Luke HEDGER *(Honda)* | 185 |
| 2 | Bradley RAY *(Honda)* | 125 |
| 3 | Catherine GREEN *(Honda)* | 118 |
| 4 | Joe IRVING *(Honda)* | 117 |
| 5 | Joe FRANCIS *(Honda)* | 108 |
| 6 | Kyle RYDE *(Honda)* | 105 |

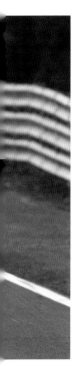

# Rapid Solicitors
# Ducati 848 Challenge

## BROWN DOMINATES

The Rapid Solicitors Ducati 848 Challenge continued for its third year with six races held alongside BSB meetings and two at stand alone events at Misano and Assen but, whilst close racing was again the order of the day, the field of riders had to play second fiddle to Cheshire's Robbie Brown who totally dominated the championship.

The former British Supersport and Virgin Cup rider took no less than seven wins and 13 podiums in the 16 races held but gained maximum points in races where guest riders crossed the line first and it all meant Brown won the title by a whopping 112 points.

It was never easy though with James Folkard, Mike Edwards and 2010 champion Darren Fry amongst his biggest challengers. Liverpool youngster Folkard improved greatly during 2012 with his highlight being a double victory at his local Oulton Park circuit whilst he also took a win at Silverstone when Brown made a rare mistake and crashed out.

Fry, who almost sat the season out due to illness, shone at Assen where he took one of the race wins and backed this up with consistent top six finishes to finish the year in third overall just ahead of Edwards. The veteran rider once again enjoyed a strong season and he was victorious at both Brands Hatch and Snetterton.

The most prominent guest riders were Lee Johnston and Chris Northover with 2008 Superstock 600 champion Johnston taking both race wins at Donington Park in September. Northover, meanwhile, enjoyed his outing at Ducati Speed Week at Misano with a first and a second.

Sam Coventry, Ed Smith and Byron Beckett all notched up consistent finishes with the former taking a brace of podiums at Assen, which helped him secure fifth in the final championship table, whilst Dennis Hobbs achieved a run of three successive third places towards the end of the year.

Northern Irishman Marty Nutt, making his debut in the series, had been expected to challenge for the title but he crashed heavily in the opening race of the season, sustaining neck and back injuries in the process. It kept him out for four months but when he returned he was an almost ever-present in the top six to set him up nicely for 2013.

The series will continue in 2013 as the Ducati 848 Challenge becomes an established feature of the British Superbike Championship. For the first time, the series comes under the organisation of MSVR with the full support of Ducati UK.

| CHAMPIONSHIP POSITIONS | | |
|---|---|---|
| 1 | Robbie BROWN | 325.5 |
| 2 | James FOLKARD | 213.5 |
| 3 | Darren FRY | 175 |
| 4 | Mike EDWARDS | 168.5 |
| 5 | Sam COVENTRY | 128 |
| 6 | Ed SMITH | 127 |

# Eastern Airways British F1 Sidecar Championship

## LOVELOCK/LAWRENCE COME OUT ON TOP

Back on the British Championship programme for a second successive year, the Eastern Airways British F1 Sidecar Championship became an official partner of BSB in 2012 and it didn't disappoint with full grids, close racing and a championship that went right down to the wire.

Roger Lovelock/Rick Lawrence and Scott Lawrie/James Neave were never more than a handful of points apart although the former held the edge in terms of both race wins and podiums. If Lawrie/Neave couldn't beat them though they invariably finished one place behind to minimise their losses and it meant both teams arrived at the final round in with a chance.

With double points on offer, there was even more at stake but it was Lovelock/Lawrence who prevailed after Lawrie/Neave retired from the first race and it was just rewards for Lovelock/Lawrence who'd led the series from the second round onwards. With four wins and twelve podiums, they ran out comfortable winners in the end with Lawrie/Neave paying for their three DNFs compared to Lovelock's one.

Ben Holland/Lee Watson were the best of the rest of the regular contenders and although they failed to take a win, they finished consistently in the top six and a run of four podiums mid season saw them finish the season in fourth overall, one place behind Lawrie/Neave.

Tim Reeves/Ashley Hawes and Jorg Steinhausen/Gregory Cluze were undoubtedly the fastest crews in the series but World Championship commitments meant they missed a number of rounds, Reeves going on to win that particular series. When they raced in Britain though, they were the teams to beat and took nine of the races between them with seven for Reeves/Hawes seeing them leap up the order in the closing stages of the season to secure second overall.

Steinhausen/Cluze opted to use the BMW engine for their challenge and although they ran into a few teething problems from time to time, the bike was fast as could be seen at Silverstone when they romped to a double victory. Five further podiums (it could have been six had they not been disqualified from Snetterton's second race) meant they ended the year in fifth overall.

The other race victors were Sean Hegarty/Calum Lawson. They missed the first four rounds of the season but took a brilliant double at Brands Hatch in July and finished on the podium in all of the other six races they finished so would certainly have been championship contenders had they competed in the full season.

Paraplegic Johan Reuterholt performed miracles all season and with Aki Aalto in the chair, scored three podiums to finish the season in an excellent sixth whilst Andy Peach/Charlie Richardson, Ben Bygrave/Paul Knapton, John Clarke/Stuart Graham, Craig Chaplow/Patrick Farrance and Steve Kershaw/Robin Wilson were always in the mix for leaderboard finishes.

### CHAMPIONSHIP POSITIONS

| | | |
|---|---|---|
| 1 | Roger LOVELOCK / Rick LAWRENCE | 343 |
| 2 | Tim REEVES / Ashley HAWES | 264 |
| 3 | Scott LAWRIE / James NEAVE | 243 |
| 4 | Ben HOLLAND / Lee WATSON | 219 |
| 5 | Jorg STEINHAUSEN / Gregory CLUZE | 194 |
| 6 | Johan REUTERHOLT / Aki AALTO | 157 |

| Name | Total | Gap | Diff | R01 Brands Hatch Indy 9 Apr | R02 Thruxton 15 Apr | R03 Oulton Park 7 May | R04 Snetterton 27 May | R05 Knockhill 24 Jun | R06 Oulton Park 8 Jul | R07 Brands Hatch GP 22 Jul | R08 Cadwell Park 27 Aug | R09 Donington Park 9 Sep | R10 TT Assen 23 Sep | R11 Silverstone 30 Sep | R12 Brands Hatch GP 14 Oct | Wins | 2nds | 3rds | Podium Credits |
|---|---|---|---|---|---|---|---|---|---|---|---|---|---|---|---|---|---|---|---|
| Shane BYRNE (Kawasaki) | 683 | | | 9 13 16 | 5 20 25 | 0 20 | 25 20 | 16 16 20 | 25 25 | 25 25 | | 25 20 | 25 20 | 20 20 | 25 25 25 | 4 | 4 | 3 | 23 |
| Josh BROOKES (Suzuki) | 655 | 28 | | 6 16 25 | 16 16 13 | 16 16 | 13 13 | 20 20 16 | 20 25 | 10 20 | 25 25 | 20 25 | 13 16 | 16 20 | 20 | 3 | 5 | 6 | 25 |
| Tommy HILL (Yamaha) | 612 | 71 | 43 | 0 20 20 | 25 13 20 | 25 0 | 20 16 | 25 25 16 | 16 16 | 25 25 | 20 16 | 20 16 | 13 9 9 | 20 10 | 16 | 7 | 5 | 4 | 35 |
| Alex LOWES (Honda) | 584 | 99 | 28 | 0 0 8 | 0 6 6 | 11 10 | 7 8 | 0 7 10 | 9 10 | 20 13 | 10 11 | 16 16 | 25 25 | | | 0 | 1 | 0 | 2 |
| Michael LAVERTY (Honda) | 581 | 102 | 3 | 0 10 3 | 10 4 9 | 20 25 | 16 25 | 0 13 11 | 13 13 | 16 16 | 16 20 | 9 9 | 16 11 | 6 16 | | 2 | 2 | 4 | 14 |
| TOMMY BRIDEWELL (BMW) | 577 | 106 | 4 | 10 5 0 | 11 9 11 | 10 0 | 11 10 | 10 9 8 | 11 9 | 7 11 | 7 13 | 10 11 | 10 13 | 9 11 | 13 | 0 | 0 | 0 | 0 |
| James WESTMORELAND (Honda) | 182 | 501 | 395 | 8 7 7 | 6 2 0 | 4 7 | 5 11 | 11 5 7 | 0 6 | 8 10 | 11 10 | 8 8 | 11 7 | 13 | 10 | 0 | 0 | 0 | 0 |
| Noriyuki HAGA (Yamaha) | 160 | 523 | 22 | 3 0 6 | 20 3 10 | 13 0 | 10 0 | 13 11 13 | 0 11 | | 0 4 | 11 10 | 1 | 8 7 | 6 | 0 | 1 | 0 | 2 |
| Chris WALKER (Kawasaki) | 138 | 545 | 22 | 4 0 1 | 9 25 7 | 9 9 | 0 0 | 9 4 5 | 10 0 | 3 5 | 8 6 | 1 2 | 6 8 | | 7 | 1 | 0 | 0 | 3 |
| Stuart EASTON (Kawasaki) | 135 | 548 | 3 | 0 11 13 | 7 11 16 | 0 8 | | | 8 0 | 0 2 | 13 9 | 7 6 | | 11 9 | 4 | 0 | 0 | 1 | 1 |
| Ian LOWRY (Honda) | 131 | 552 | 4 | 13 25 11 | 0 0 3 | 8 13 | 0 6 | 0 10 9 | 0 8 | 4 9 | 0 0 | 2 | 7 3 | | | 1 | 0 | 0 | 3 |
| Jon KIRKHAM (Honda) | 122 | 561 | 9 | 25 9 9 | 9 9 0 | 0 2 | 4 2 | 0 0 2 | 4 2 | 11 4 | 9 7 | 3 | 4 2 | 7 8 | 8 | 1 | 0 | 0 | 3 |
| Alastair SEELEY (Suzuki) | 95 | 558 | 27 | 20 1 0 | 13 10 5 | 0 0 | 9 9 | 0 8 3 | 7 5 | 2 3 | 0 0 | | | | | 0 | 1 | 0 | 2 |
| Barry BURRELL (BMW) | 84 | 599 | 11 | 0 2 0 | 0 0 0 | 6 0 | 0 5 | 6 0 0 | 0 0 | 1 6 | 3 4 | 4 4 | 5 | 10 13 | 11 | 0 | 0 | 0 | 0 |
| Luca SCASSA (Honda) | 76 | 607 | 8 | 0 8 10 | 3 0 0 | 0 0 | 8 7 | 6 7 6 | 0 7 | 2 0 | 1 0 | 6 3 | 13 5 | 8 10 | 1 2 | 0 | 0 | 0 | 0 |
| Graeme GOWLAND (Honda) | 69 | 614 | 7 | 0 6 2 | 0 1 8 | 0 11 | 8 7 | 7 6 6 | 0 7 | | | | | | | 0 | 0 | 0 | 0 |
| Peter HICKMAN (Kawasaki/BMW) | 65 | 618 | 4 | 0 0 4 | 0 5 0 | | 0 3 | 8 3 4 | 0 0 | 6 8 | 0 1 | | 2 6 | 6 9 | 0 0 | 0 | 0 | 0 | 0 |
| Patrick MUFF (BMW) | 63 | 620 | 2 | 0 0 0 | 4 8 2 | 7 6 | 1 0 | 5 2 0 | 1 1 | 0 0 | 4 5 | 5 3 | 1 | 5 | 3 | 0 | 0 | 0 | 0 |
| Michael RUTTER (Kawasaki) | 61 | 622 | 2 | 16 0 0 | 8 0 1 | 2 3 | 6 0 | 2 0 0 | 6 0 | 5 6 | 0 2 | | | 3 | 1 | 0 | 0 | 1 | 1 |
| Dan Linfoot (BMW) | 30 | 653 | 31 | 0 4 5 | 1 7 4 | 5 5 | | | | | | | | | | 0 | 0 | 0 | 0 |
| Karl HARRIS (Kawasaki) | 23 | 660 | 7 | | | | | | | 3 4 | 9 7 | | 3 | 4 | | 0 | 0 | 0 | 0 |
| Robbin HARMS (Honda) | 23 | 660 | 0 | | | | | | | 0 0 | 1 0 | 6 7 | 5 | 4 | | 0 | 0 | 0 | 0 |
| Luke QUIGLEY (Honda) | 18 | 665 | 5 | 0 0 0 | 2 0 0 | 3 4 | 2 1 | 4 0 0 | 0 0 | 0 0 | 2 0 | | | | | 0 | 0 | 0 | 0 |
| Danny BUCHAN (Kawasaki) | 16 | 667 | 2 | | | | | | | 0 0 | 13 0 | 3 0 | | | | 0 | 0 | 0 | 0 |
| Gary MASON (Kawasaki) | 14 | 669 | 2 | 11 3 0 | 0 0 0 | 0 0 | | | 0 0 | 0 0 | | | | | | 0 | 0 | 0 | 0 |
| Jason O'HALLORAN (Honda) | 10 | 673 | 4 | | | | | | | | | | | 5 5 | | 0 | 0 | 0 | 0 |
| Tristan PALMER (Honda) | 8 | 675 | 2 | 0 0 0 | 0 0 0 | 1 0 | 3 4 | 0 0 0 | 0 0 | 0 0 | | | | | | 0 | 0 | 0 | 0 |
| Scott SMART (Ducati) | 8 | 675 | 0 | 2 0 0 | 0 0 0 | 0 1 | 0 0 | 3 1 1 | 0 0 | 0 0 | 0 0 | | | | | 0 | 0 | 0 | 0 |
| Jakub SMRZ (Aprilia) | 8 | 675 | 0 | | | | | | | | | | 1 | 4 | 1 2 | 0 | 0 | 0 | 0 |
| Freddy FORAY (Kawasaki) | 7 | 676 | 1 | 7 0 0 | 0 0 0 | 0 0 | 0 0 | 0 0 | 0 0 | | | | | | | 0 | 0 | 0 | 0 |
| Alex POLITA (Ducati) | 5 | 678 | 2 | 2 5 0 | 0 0 0 | 0 0 | | | | 0 0 | | | | | | 0 | 0 | 0 | 0 |
| Mark AITCHISON (Aprilia) | 3 | 680 | 2 | | | | | | 1 0 | 0 0 | 0 0 | | 2 | | | 0 | 0 | 0 | 0 |
| John LAVERTY (Aprilia) | 3 | 680 | 0 | 0 0 0 | 0 0 0 | 0 0 | 0 0 | 0 0 0 | 0 0 | 0 0 | 0 0 | | 3 | | | 0 | 0 | 0 | 0 |
| James HILLIER (Kawasaki) | 1 | 682 | 2 | 1 0 0 | 0 0 0 | 0 0 | 0 0 | | | 0 0 | | | | | | 0 | 0 | 0 | 0 |
| Florian MARINO (Aprilia) | 0 | 683 | 1 | 0 0 0 | 0 0 0 | 0 0 | 0 0 | 0 0 0 | 0 0 | | | | | | | 0 | 0 | 0 | 0 |
| Aaron ZANOTTI (Suzuki) | 0 | 683 | 0 | 0 0 0 | 0 0 0 | 0 0 | 0 0 | 0 0 0 | 0 0 | 0 0 | 0 0 | | | | | 0 | 0 | 0 | 0 |
| Jennie TINMOUTH (Kawasaki) | 0 | 683 | 0 | 0 0 0 | 0 0 0 | 0 0 | 0 0 | 0 0 0 | 0 0 | 0 0 | 0 0 | | | | | 0 | 0 | 0 | 0 |
| Tom TUNSTALL (Honda) | 0 | 683 | 0 | 0 0 0 | 0 0 0 | 0 0 | 0 0 | 0 0 0 | 0 0 | 0 0 | 0 0 | | | | | 0 | 0 | 0 | 0 |
| Abdulaziz BINLADEN (Ducati) | 0 | 683 | 0 | 0 0 0 | 0 0 0 | 0 0 | 0 0 | 0 0 0 | 0 0 | 0 0 | 0 0 | | | | | 0 | 0 | 0 | 0 |
| Keith FARMER (Kawasaki) | 0 | 683 | 0 | | | | | | | 0 0 | 0 0 | | | | | 0 | 0 | 0 | 0 |
| David ANTHONY (Honda) | 0 | 683 | 0 | | | | | | | 0 0 | 0 0 | | | | | 0 | 0 | 0 | 0 |
| Tom GRANT (Kawasaki) | 0 | 683 | 0 | | | | | | | | | | 0 0 | 0 0 | 0 | 0 | 0 | 0 | 0 |
| Troy HERFOSS (Aprilia) | 0 | 683 | 0 | | | | | | | | | | | | | 0 | 0 | 0 | 0 |
| Victor COX (Kawasaki) | 0 | 683 | 0 | | | | | | | | | | | | | 0 | 0 | 0 | 0 |

# Manufacturers Championship
Points after final round

| Name | Total | Gap | Diff | R01 | R02 | R03 | R04 | R05 | R06 | R07 | R08 | R09 | R10 | R11 | R12 |
|---|---|---|---|---|---|---|---|---|---|---|---|---|---|---|---|
| Kawasaki | 482 | | | 16 13 16 | 9 25 25 | 9 20 | 25 20 | 16 16 20 | 25 25 | 13 7 | 13 9 | 25 20 | 20 20 | 25 25 25 | |
| Suzuki | 470 | 12 | | 20 16 25 | 16 16 13 | 16 16 | 13 13 | 20 20 16 | 20 25 | 10 20 | 25 25 | 20 25 | 13 16 | 16 20 20 | |
| Yamaha | 443 | 39 | 27 | 3 20 20 | 25 13 20 | 25 | 20 16 | 25 25 25 | 16 16 | 25 25 | 20 16 | 11 13 | 9 9 | 20 10 16 | |
| Honda | 426 | 56 | 17 | 25 25 11 | 10 6 9 | 20 25 | 16 25 | 11 13 11 | 13 13 | 20 16 | 16 20 | 25 25 | 13 16 | 16 16 | |
| BMW | 253 | 229 | 173 | 10 5 5 | 11 9 11 | 10 6 | 11 10 | 10 9 8 | 11 9 | 7 11 | 7 13 | 10 11 | 10 13 | 10 13 13 | |
| Aprilia | 9 | 473 | 244 | | | | | | | | | | 1 | 4 | 2 2 |
| Ducati | 8 | 474 | 1 | 5 | | | | 1 | | 1 1 | | | | | |

# MCE British Superbike Championship with Pirelli
Speedy fastest lap league points after final round

| Name | Total | Gap | Diff | R01 | R02 | R03 | R04 | R05 | R06 | R07 | R08 | R09 | R10 | R11 | R12 |
|---|---|---|---|---|---|---|---|---|---|---|---|---|---|---|---|
| Josh BROOKES (Suzuki) | 8 | | | | 1 | | | | 1 | 1 | 1 | | 1 1 | 1 | 1 1 |
| Tommy HILL (Yamaha) | 6 | 2 | | | | 1 | | 1 | | 1 | | 2 | | | |
| Alex LOWES (Honda) | 5 | 3 | 1 | | 1 | | | 1 | | | 1 | | | 1 1 | |
| Michael LAVERTY (Honda) | 3 | 5 | 2 | | | | 1 1 | 1 | | | | | | | |
| Shane BYRNE (Kawasaki) | 2 | 6 | 1 | | | | 1 | | | 1 | | | | | |
| Alastair SEELEY (Suzuki) | 1 | 7 | 1 | 1 | | | | | | | | | | | |
| Graeme GOWLAND (Honda) | 1 | 7 | 0 | | | 1 | | | | | | | | | |
| Tommy Bridewell (BMW) | 1 | 7 | 0 | | | | | | | | | | | 1 | |

# Motorpoint British Supersport Championship
## Riders points after final round

| Name | Total | Gap | Diff | R01 Brands Hatch Indy 9 Apr | | R02 Thruxton 15 Apr | | R03 Oulton Park 7 May | | R04 Snetterton 27 May | | R05 Knockhill 24 Jun | | R06 Oulton Park 8 Jul | | R07 Brands Hatch GP 22 Jul | | R08 Cadwell Park 27 Aug | | R09 Donington Park 9 Sep | | R10 TT Circuit Assen 23 Sep | | R11 Silverstone 30 Sep | | R12 Brands Hatch GP 14 Oct | |
|---|---|---|---|---|---|---|---|---|---|---|---|---|---|---|---|---|---|---|---|---|---|---|---|---|---|---|---|
| Glen RICHARDS | 372 | | | | 4 | 25 | 16 | 13 | 25 | 20 | 16 | 25 | 20 | | 25 | 25 | 20 | 16 | 25 | | 25 | 10 | 16 | 20 | 10 | 16 | |
| Jack KENNEDY | 363.5 | 8.5 | | 10 | 12.5 | 13 | 20 | 25 | 16 | 25 | 25 | 20 | 16 | | 16 | 20 | 25 | 13 | 9 | 25 | 20 | 20 | | | 13 | 20 | |
| Billy MCCONNELL | 340 | 32 | 23.5 | 7 | 8 | | 25 | 11 | 9 | 11 | 20 | 13 | 25 | 25 | 20 | | 16 | 25 | 13 | 20 | 13 | 4 | 6 | 13 | 6 | 25 | 25 |
| Christian IDDON | 285.5 | 86.5 | 54.5 | 13 | 6.5 | 10 | 6 | 10 | 11 | 9 | 11 | 9 | | | | 16 | 13 | 20 | 20 | 16 | 16 | 25 | 20 | 25 | 16 | 13 | |
| Ben WILSON | 259 | 113 | 26.5 | 20 | | 16 | 11 | 20 | 20 | 16 | | 5 | 13 | 20 | 13 | 10 | 11 | 10 | | | | 9 | 9 | 11 | 25 | 9 | 11 |
| Richard COOPER | 221 | 151 | 38 | 4 | 5 | 8 | 7 | 9 | 10 | | | 11 | 10 | | | 10 | 16 | | | 10 | | 16 | 11 | 16 | 20 | 11 | 20 |
| Luke MOSSEY | 172 | 200 | 49 | | | 11 | 13 | 8 | 7 | 13 | | 10 | 11 | 16 | 11 | 11 | 8 | 11 | 11 | 11 | | 13 | 7 | | | | |
| Pauli PEKKANEN | 159 | 213 | 13 | 16 | | 9 | 8 | 7 | 8 | | 8 | 8 | 9 | 13 | 9 | 9 | 9 | 8 | 8 | 9 | 9 | 5 | | 7 | | | |
| Glenn IRWIN | 153 | 219 | 6 | 11 | | 4 | 9 | 6 | 6 | 7 | 10 | 6 | | 10 | 6 | | 5 | 7 | 7 | 13 | 11 | 8 | 10 | 9 | | 8 | |
| Luke JONES | 141.5 | 230.5 | 11.5 | | 4.5 | 6 | 10 | 5 | 3 | 8 | | 7 | 8 | 7 | | 13 | | | | 8 | 8 | 3 | 8 | 8 | 9 | 10 | 16 |
| Sam WARREN | 138 | 234 | 3.5 | 25 | 10 | | | 16 | 13 | 10 | 13 | 16 | | | | 6 | | 9 | | | | | | | | | |
| Dean HIPWELL | 69 | 303 | 69 | 8 | 2 | 3 | 4 | | 1 | 1 | | | 4 | 5 | 1 | 3 | 4 | | 5 | 5 | 5 | | 1 | 4 | 3 | 4 | 6 |
| Deane BROWN | 64.5 | 307.5 | 4.5 | | 5.5 | | | 3 | | | | 3 | 7 | 8 | 4 | 8 | | 6 | | 10 | | 2 | | | | | 8 |
| Taylor MACKENZIE | 63 | 309 | 1.5 | | | | | | | | | 5 | | 5 | 4 | 2 | 2 | 2 | 2 | 3 | 1 | 7 | 7 | 8 | | 6 | 10 |
| Nikki COATES | 56 | 316 | 7 | | | 2 | 1 | 1 | 2 | 4 | 9 | 2 | | 9 | 3 | 5 | 6 | | 4 | | 4 | | 2 | | 2 | | |
| James EAST | 55 | 317 | 1 | 5 | 3 | | | | | | | 1 | 3 | 2 | | 4 | 7 | 5 | | | | 6 | 5 | 5 | | 5 | 9 |
| Kev COGHLAN | 54.5 | 317.5 | 0.5 | 3 | 3.5 | 7 | 5 | 2 | 5 | 6 | | 4 | | 11 | 8 | | | | | | | | | | | | |
| Graeme GOWLAND | 41 | 331 | 13.5 | | | | | | | | | | | | | | | | | | | 10 | 11 | 7 | | 13 | |
| Sam HORNSEY | 37 | 335 | 4 | 2 | 1 | | | 3 | | | | | 5 | 7 | | | | 6 | 6 | | | 3 | 4 | | | | |
| Jimmy HILL | 32.5 | 339.5 | 4.5 | 9 | 0.5 | 5 | 3 | 4 | 4 | 5 | | | 2 | | | | | | | | | | | | | | |
| PJ JACOBSEN | 32 | 340 | 0.5 | | | | | | | | | | | | | | | | | | | 7 | 25 | | | | |
| Daniel COOPER | 28.5 | 343.5 | 3.5 | 6 | 2.5 | | | | | | | 6 | | 6 | 5 | | | 3 | | | | | | | | | |
| Brodie WATERS | 27 | 345 | 1.5 | | | | | | | | | | | | | | | | | | | | | 5 | 7 | 3 | 7 |
| Raymond SCHOUTEN | 24 | 348 | 3 | | | | | | | | | | | | | | | | | | | 11 | 13 | | | | |
| Luke STAPLEFORD | 20.5 | 351.5 | 3.5 | 1 | 1.5 | 1 | | | | | | | | | | 4 | 6 | 3 | 1 | | | | | 2 | 1 | | |
| David PATON | 19 | 353 | 1.5 | | | | | | | 2 | 7 | | | | | 1 | 1 | | | | | 1 | 4 | | | | 3 |
| Ben FIELD | 13 | 359 | 6 | | | | | | | 6 | | | | | | | | 4 | 3 | | | | | | | | |
| Shaun WINFIELD | 9 | 363 | 4 | | | | | | | | | | | | | | | 2 | | | | | | 2 | | 2 | 5 |
| John SIMPSON | 8 | 364 | 1 | | | | | | | | | | | | | | | | | | | 3 | | 1 | | | 4 |
| Josh CAYGILL | 6 | 366 | 2 | | | | | | | 4 | | | | | | | | 2 | | | | | | | | | |
| Johnathan LODGE | 6 | 366 | 0 | | | | | | | | | | | 1 | | | | 1 | | 2 | | | | | | | |
| Matt LYAT | 5 | 367 | 1 | | | | | | | 3 | | | | | | | | | 2 | | | | | | | | |
| Scott HUDSON | 4 | 368 | 1 | | | | | | | | | | | | | | | | 3 | | | | | | | | 1 |
| Philip ATKINSON | 3 | 369 | 1 | | | | | | | | | | | 3 | | | | | | | | | | | | | |
| Craig NEVE | 3 | 369 | 0 | | | | | | | 2 | | | | | | | | | | | | | | 1 | | | |
| Adam BLACKLOCK | 2 | 370 | 1 | | | | 2 | | | | | | | | | | | | | | | | | | | | |
| Gary WINFIELD | 1 | 371 | 1 | | | | | | | 1 | | | | | | | | | | | | | | | | | |
| David JONES | 1 | 371 | 0 | | | | | | | | | 1 | | | | | | | | | | | | | | | |
| Tom McHALE | 1 | 371 | 0 | | | | | | | | | | | | | | | | | | | 1 | | | | | |

# Motorpoint British Supersport Championship
## Cup points after final round

| Name | Total | Gap | Diff | R01 | | R02 | | R03 | | R04 | | R05 | | R06 | | R07 | | R08 | | R09 | | R10 | | R11 | | R12 | |
|---|---|---|---|---|---|---|---|---|---|---|---|---|---|---|---|---|---|---|---|---|---|---|---|---|---|---|---|
| Glenn IRWIN | 388 | | | 25 | | 20 | 20 | 25 | 25 | 20 | 25 | 20 | 13 | 25 | 20 | | 20 | 25 | 25 | 25 | 25 | 25 | 25 | 25 | | 20 | |
| Luke JONES | 365 | 23 | | | 12.5 | 25 | 25 | 20 | 20 | 25 | | 25 | 25 | | 25 | 25 | | | | 20 | 20 | 20 | 20 | 20 | 25 | 25 | 25 |
| Jonathan LODGE | 230 | 158 | 135 | | 5 | 11 | 11 | 11 | 11 | | | | | 13 | 13 | 13 | 16 | 16 | 16 | | 13 | 13 | 11 | 16 | 13 | 13 | 20 |
| James EAST | 227 | 161 | 3 | 20 | 10 | 16 | 16 | | 16 | 16 | | 16 | 20 | 16 | 16 | 20 | 25 | 20 | | | | | | | | | |
| Matt LYAT | 215 | 173 | 12 | | | 13 | 13 | 16 | 13 | 10 | 16 | | | 9 | 10 | 11 | 11 | 13 | 20 | 8 | 10 | 11 | 10 | 10 | 11 | | |
| Ben FIELD | 192 | 196 | 23 | | | | | 10 | 9 | 13 | 20 | | | 11 | 11 | 16 | 13 | | | 16 | 16 | 10 | 16 | 11 | 20 | | |
| Craig NEVE | 142.5 | 245.5 | 49.5 | 16 | 5.5 | 8 | | 8 | 7 | | 13 | | | | 9 | | | 11 | | 10 | | 9 | 9 | 13 | 16 | 16 | |
| Gary WINFIELD | 138 | 250 | 4.5 | | | | | | | 9 | 11 | 13 | 16 | 8 | | | | 10 | 13 | 9 | 8 | 7 | 7 | | 9 | 8 | 10 |
| Jodie LEES | 52 | 336 | 86 | | 8 | | | 13 | 10 | 11 | | | | 10 | | | | | | | | | | | | | |
| Mark DAVIES | 38 | 350 | 14 | | | | | | | | | | | | | | | 11 | 11 | 8 | 8 | | | | | | |
| Robbie STEWART | 36 | 352 | 2 | | | | | | | | | | | | | | | | | | | | | 9 | 10 | 4 | 13 |
| Dan STEWART | 29 | 359 | 7 | | | | | | | | | | | | | | | | | | | 16 | 13 | | | 10 | 16 |
| David HAIRE | 26 | 362 | 3 | | | | | | | | | | | | | | | | | | | | | | | 10 | 16 |
| Tom McHALE | 22 | 366 | 4 | | | | | | | | | | | | | | | 13 | 9 | | | | | | | | |
| Philip ATKINSON | 20 | 368 | 2 | | | | | | | | | | | 20 | | | | | | | | | | | | | |
| Martin VAN RUITENBEEK | 20 | 368 | 0 | | | | | | | | | | | | | | | | | | | | | | | 9 | 11 |
| Sam COVENTRY | 17 | 371 | 3 | | | | | | | 9 | 8 | | | | | | | | | | | | | | | | |
| Anthony ROGERS | 16.5 | 371.5 | 0.5 | | 6.5 | | 10 | | | | | | | | | | | | | | | | | | | | |
| Daniel BRAY | 16 | 372 | 0.5 | | | 7 | 9 | | | | | | | | | | | | | | | | | | | | |
| Alex BARKSHIRE | 10 | 378 | 6 | | | 10 | | | | | | | | | | | | | | | | | | | | | |
| Jess TRAYLOR | 9 | 379 | 1 | | | 9 | | | | | | | | | | | | | | | | | | | | | |

# Motorpoint British Supersport Championship
## Speedy fastest lap league points after round 23

| Name | Total | Gap | Diff | | | | | | | | | | | | | | | | | | | | | | | | |
|---|---|---|---|---|---|---|---|---|---|---|---|---|---|---|---|---|---|---|---|---|---|---|---|---|---|---|---|
| Glen RICHARDS | 9 | | | | | | | 1 | | 1 | | | | 1 | 2 | | | 2 | | | | 2 | | | | | |
| Christian IDDON | 5 | 4 | | | | | | | | | | 1 | 2 | | | | | | | | | 2 | | | | | |
| Jack KENNEDY | 5 | 4 | 0 | | | | | | | 1 | | | | 1 | | | | | | 2 | | 1 | | | | | |
| Billy McCONNELL | 5 | 4 | 0 | | | | | | | | | 1 | | | | 1 | | | | 2 | | | | | | | 1 |
| Ben WILSON | 3 | 6 | 2 | | | 1 | | | | 2 | | | | | | | | | | | | | | | | | |
| Sam WARREN | 2 | 7 | 1 | 1 | | | 1 | | | | | | | | | | | | | | | | | | | | |
| Richard COOPER | 2 | 7 | 0 | | | | | | | | | | | | | | | | | | | | | 1 | | 1 | |
| Luke MOSSEY | 1 | 8 | 1 | | | | | | | | | | | | | | | | | 1 | | | | | | | |

# Metzeler National Superstock 1000 Championship
Riders points after final round

| Name | Total | Gap | Diff | Brands Hatch Indy 9 April 2012 | Thruxton 15 April 2012 | Oulton Park 7 May 2012 | Donington - Race 1 13 May 2012 | Donington - Race 2 13 May 2012 | Snetterton 27 May 2012 | Knockhill 24 June 2012 | Oulton Park 8 July 2012 | Brands Hatch GP 22 July 2012 | Cadwell Park 27 August 2012 | Donington Park 9 September 2012 | Silverstone 30 September 2012 | Brands Hatch GP 14 October 2012 |
|---|---|---|---|---|---|---|---|---|---|---|---|---|---|---|---|---|
| Keith FARMER | 207 | | | 25 | 25 | | | 10 | 9 | 11 | 25 | 16 | 20 | 25 | 16 | 25 |
| Jason O'HALLORAN | 157 | 50 | | 16 | 16 | | 25 | | 10 | 25 | | 13 | 25 | 16 | 11 | |
| Victor COX | 142 | 65 | 15 | 7 | 13 | 8 | 13 | 7 | 5 | 16 | 20 | 11 | 5 | 16 | 10 | 11 |
| Jimmy STORRAR | 117 | 90 | 25 | 11 | | 20 | 20 | 20 | | | 20 | 7 | 7 | 4 | 8 | |
| Lee COSTELLO | 114 | 93 | 3 | 6 | 6 | 9 | 11 | 13 | | 5 | 6 | 9 | 11 | 13 | 25 | |
| Howie MAINWARING | 105 | 102 | 9 | 4 | 20 | 13 | | | | | 9 | 11 | 13 | 10 | 9 | 16 |
| Steve BROGAN | 98 | 109 | 7 | 20 | | 11 | | | 25 | 13 | 11 | 10 | 1 | 7 | | |
| David JOHNSON | 90 | 117 | 8 | 5 | 10 | 16 | 10 | 11 | | 13 | 25 | | | | | |
| Adam JENKINSON | 90 | 117 | 0 | | 13 | 9 | | | 8 | 9 | 6 | 16 | 13 | 9 | 7 | |
| Danny BUCHAN | 85 | 122 | 5 | | | 8 | 25 | 16 | 16 | 20 | | | | | | |
| PJ JACOBSEN | 84 | 123 | 1 | | | | | | | | | 9 | 10 | 25 | 20 | 20 |
| Gary JOHNSON | 59 | 148 | 25 | | 10 | 10 | | | | 8 | 4 | 6 | 6 | 6 | 4 | 5 |
| Jonathan RAILTON | 58 | 149 | 1 | | 11 | 6 | 7 | | 8 | 1 | 3 | | 8 | 3 | 11 | |
| Daniel JOHNSON | 55 | 152 | 3 | | 3 | 5 | 3 | 1 | 10 | 1 | | | 8 | 8 | 6 | 10 |
| Patrick MEDCALF | 50 | 157 | 5 | 1 | | | 9 | | 6 | 16 | 1 | 7 | | | 1 | 9 |
| Joe BURNS | 33 | 174 | 17 | | | | | | | | | | 20 | | 13 | |
| John MCGUINNESS | 30 | 177 | 3 | | | 7 | | | | 10 | 2 | 3 | | | | 8 |
| Lee JOHNSTON | 25 | 182 | 5 | | | | | | | | | 5 | | 20 | | |
| Freddie RUSSO | 25 | 182 | 0 | | 8 | 5 | 1 | | 6 | 5 | | | | | | |
| Hudson KENNAUGH | 25 | 182 | 0 | 3 | | | | 5 | 4 | | | | | | | 13 |
| Joshua DAY | 18 | 189 | 7 | 2 | | 3 | | | 6 | 7 | | | | | | |
| Conor CUMMINS | 15 | 192 | 3 | 9 | | 4 | 2 | | | | | | | | | |
| John INGRAM | 14 | 193 | 1 | | | | | | | | | | 9 | 5 | | |
| Josh ELLIOTT | 14 | 193 | 0 | | | | 4 | | 8 | | 2 | | | | | |
| Marshall NEILL | 11 | 196 | 3 | | | | | | 4 | 4 | 3 | | | | | |
| Joe DICKINSON | 10 | 197 | 1 | | 1 | | 8 | | | | | | | 1 | | |
| Ashley BEECH | 9 | 198 | 1 | | | | 2 | 7 | | | | | | | | |
| Cody NALLY | 9 | 198 | 0 | | | | | | | | 5 | 4 | | | | |
| Jesse TRAYLER | 9 | 198 | 0 | | | | | | | | 4 | 2 | | | | 3 |
| James HILLIER | 7 | 200 | 2 | | | | | | | | | | | | | 7 |
| Gavin HUNT | 7 | 200 | 0 | 7 | | | | | | | | | | | | |
| Peter WARD | 6 | 201 | 1 | | | | | | | | | | | | | 6 |
| Paul CURRAN | 6 | 201 | 0 | | | | | | | | | | | | 5 | 1 |
| Mike BOOTH | 6 | 201 | 0 | | | 2 | | | | 1 | 3 | | | | | |
| Leon MORRIS | 5 | 202 | 1 | | | | | | | | 2 | | | 3 | | |
| Gerrard KINGHAN | 5 | 202 | 0 | 2 | 3 | | | | | | | | | | | |
| Rob McNEALY | 5 | 202 | 0 | | | 3 | | | | | | | | | | 2 |
| Dominic USHER | 4 | 203 | 1 | | | | | | | | | | | | | 4 |
| Dan KNEEN | 4 | 203 | 0 | 4 | | | | | | | | | | | | |
| Leon HUNT | 4 | 203 | 0 | 2 | 2 | | | | | | | | | | | |
| Jonathan HOWARTH | 2 | 205 | 2 | | | | | | | | | | | | 2 | |
| Dean BROWN | 1 | 206 | 1 | 1 | | | | | | | | | | | | |

# Metzeler National Superstock 600 Championship
Riders points after final round

| Name | Total | Gap | Diff | Brands Hatch Indy 9 April 2012 | Thruxton 15 April 2012 | Oulton Park 7 May 2012 | Donington - Race 1 13 May 2012 | Donington - Race 2 13 May 2012 | Snetterton 27 May 2012 | Knockhill 24 June 2012 | Oulton Park 8 July 2012 | Brands Hatch GP 22 July 2012 | Cadwell Park 27 August 2012 | Donington Park 9 September 2012 | Silverstone 30 September 2012 | Brands Hatch GP 14 October 2012 |
|---|---|---|---|---|---|---|---|---|---|---|---|---|---|---|---|---|
| Lee JACKSON | 199 | | | | 6 | 11 | 13 | 16 | 16 | 7 | 25 | 10 | 25 | 25 | 20 | 25 |
| Ben BURKE | 174 | 25 | | | 11 | 10 | 20 | 25 | 25 | 25 | 16 | 13 | 9 | 20 | | |
| James ROSE | 169 | 30 | 5 | 20 | 20 | | 11 | 20 | 20 | | 13 | 10 | 16 | 16 | 10 | 13 |
| Jake DIXON | 135 | 64 | 34 | 25 | 16 | 13 | 16 | | | | | 2 | 13 | 25 | 25 | |
| Alex OLSEN | 105 | 94 | 30 | | | 20 | 25 | 13 | | | | 8 | 10 | 13 | 16 | |
| Josh WAINWRIGHT | 98 | 101 | 7 | 13 | 10 | | | | | 7 | 8 | 7 | 11 | 16 | 10 | 16 |
| James LODGE | 97 | 102 | 1 | 16 | 5 | | | 7 | 9 | 5 | 20 | 20 | | | 8 | 7 |
| Johnny BLACKSHAW | 91 | 108 | 6 | 4 | 13 | | | | 11 | 10 | 16 | 9 | 9 | | | 8 |
| Grant WHITAKER | 83 | 116 | 1 | 8 | 11 | 7 | 25 | 5 | 7 | | 9 | | 7 | 4 | | |
| Tom FISHER | 81 | 118 | 2 | 10 | 8 | 7 | | | 10 | 13 | 10 | 11 | 1 | 5 | 6 | |
| Tim HASTINGS | 66 | 133 | 15 | 6 | 25 | 2 | | | 6 | 11 | 5 | | | | | 11 |
| Joe COLLIER | 65 | 134 | 1 | | | 2 | | | | 3 | | | 20 | 9 | 11 | 20 |
| Bjorn ESTMENT | 64 | 135 | 1 | | | 3 | 4 | 10 | | 9 | 7 | | 6 | 8 | 7 | 10 |
| Matthew PAULO | 51 | 148 | 13 | 2 | | 9 | | 8 | | | 11 | 4 | 11 | 1 | | 5 |
| Jordan SIMPKIN | 38 | 161 | 13 | 3 | | 4 | 6 | | | 6 | 6 | | 5 | 8 | | |
| Niall CAMPBELL | 34 | 165 | 4 | | | | 16 | 6 | 5 | | 4 | 3 | | | | |
| Leon JEACOCK | 34 | 165 | 0 | | 9 | | 9 | | 2 | | 8 | | | | 2 | 4 |
| Michael ROBERTSON | 32 | 167 | 2 | | | | | | | | | 20 | 5 | 7 | | |
| Kyle WILKS | 31 | 168 | 1 | | | | | 2 | | 4 | | | 3 | | 9 | 13 |
| Mark WILKINSON | 28 | 171 | 3 | | | 1 | 3 | | 1 | 1 | | 6 | 2 | 1 | 6 | 1 |
| Ben GRINDROD | 23 | 176 | 5 | | | | | | | | | | 13 | 1 | 1 | 9 |
| Daniel MURPHY | 18 | 181 | 5 | | | | 9 | 4 | | | | | | 5 | | |
| Scott HUDSON | 16 | 183 | 2 | 7 | | | 1 | 8 | | | | | | | | |
| Nick ANDERSON | 13 | 186 | 3 | 3 | 5 | | 3 | 3 | | | | | 2 | | | |
| Daniel KINLOCH | 12 | 187 | 1 | | | | 5 | 4 | | | 3 | | | | | |
| Jake NEWSTEAD | 11 | 188 | 1 | | | | | | | | 1 | | 3 | 3 | 4 | |
| Jack GROVES | 10 | 189 | 1 | | | 8 | | | | | | | 2 | | | |
| Tommy DALE | 9 | 190 | 1 | | | | | | | | | | 4 | 2 | 3 | |
| John Dean | 8 | 191 | 1 | 8 | | | | | | | | | | | | |
| Ben GODFREY | 7 | 192 | 1 | | | | | | | | | | | | 5 | 2 |
| James PHARE | 7 | 192 | 0 | | | | | | | | | 4 | | | | 3 |
| James RISPOLI | 6 | 193 | 1 | | | | | | | | | | | | | 6 |
| Jamie PERRIN | 2 | 197 | 4 | | | | | | 2 | | | | | | | |
| Jamie HARRIS | 1 | 198 | 1 | | | | | | | | 1 | | | | | |
| Tom YOUNG | 1 | 198 | 0 | | | 1 | | | | | | | | | | |
| Piers HUTCHINS | 1 | 198 | 0 | 1 | | | | | | | | | | | | |

# Monster Energy British Motostar Championship & Motostar Cup
Riders points after final round

| Name | Total | Gap | Diff | Thruxton - Brands Race 14 April 2012 | Thruxton 15 April 2012 | Oulton Park 7 May 2012 | Snetterton 27 May 2012 | Knockhill 24 June 2012 | Oulton Park 8 July 2012 | Brands Hatch GP 22 July 2012 | Cadwell Park 27 August 2012 | Donington Park 9 September 2012 | TT Circuit Assen 23 September 2012 | Silverstone 30 September 2012 | Brands Hatch GP 14 October 2012 |
|---|---|---|---|---|---|---|---|---|---|---|---|---|---|---|---|
| Luke HEDGER | 185 | | | 13 | 20 | 25 | 16 | | 25 | 20 | 10 | 13 | 10 | 13 | 20 |
| Bradley RAY | 125 | 60 | | 25 | 25 | | | | | 25 | | 25 | | | 25 |
| Catherine GREEN | 118 | 67 | 7 | 3 | 7 | | 10 | 16 | | 13 | 25 | 20 | 11 | | 13 |
| Joe IRVING | 117 | 68 | 1 | 11 | 10 | | 11 | | 7 | 11 | 16 | 10 | 16 | 16 | 9 |
| Joe FRANCIS | 108 | 77 | 9 | 9 | 8 | 9 | 6 | 10 | 13 | 8 | 20 | | | 9 | 16 |
| Kyle RYDE | 105 | 80 | 3 | 20 | | | 25 | 25 | | | | | 25 | | 10 |
| Jordan WEAVING | 99 | 86 | 6 | 16 | 16 | | 20 | | | | | 16 | 20 | | 11 |
| Tom CARNE | 87 | 98 | 12 | 8 | 6 | 7 | 7 | 11 | 11 | 5 | 4 | | | 20 | 8 |
| Philip WAKEFIELD | 84 | 101 | 3 | | | | 8 | 13 | 20 | 10 | 8 | 6 | 8 | 11 | |
| Tarran MACKENZIE | 76 | 109 | 8 | | | | | 9 | 20 | | | 16 | 11 | 13 | 7 |
| Callum BEY | 73 | 112 | 3 | 4 | | 3 | 6 | 4 | 9 | 9 | 9 | 9 | 9 | 6 | 5 |
| Ryan WATSON | 71 | 114 | 2 | | 13 | 20 | 13 | 8 | 1 | 6 | 6 | 2 | | | 2 |
| Harry HARTLEY | 60 | 125 | 11 | 7 | 2 | | 11 | 5 | 3 | 10 | 3 | 11 | 8 | | |
| Amie SHELTON | 50 | 135 | 10 | | | | 8 | 3 | 5 | 6 | 7 | 13 | 3 | 5 | |
| Bradley HUGHES | 39 | 146 | 11 | 6 | 5 | | 10 | 1 | 4 | 4 | 4 | | | 5 | |
| William DUNLOP | 35 | 150 | 4 | 10 | 9 | | 16 | | | | | | | | |
| Harry STAFFORD | 25 | 160 | 10 | | | | | | | | | | | 25 | |
| Ollie SIMPSON | 23 | 162 | 2 | | | | | | | | | 7 | 9 | 7 | |
| Tommy PHILIP | 22 | 163 | 1 | 2 | | 4 | 4 | | 1 | | 1 | 7 | 3 | | |
| Xavier ZAYAT | 22 | 163 | 0 | 1 | | | | 2 | 6 | 3 | | 5 | 2 | 3 | |
| Peter SUTHERLAND | 21 | 164 | 1 | | 1 | | | | 2 | | | | 4 | 6 | 8 |
| Connoe BEHAN | 16 | 169 | 5 | | | | | | | 16 | | | | | |
| Anthony ALONSO | 14 | 171 | 2 | | | | | | | | | | | 10 | 4 |
| Elliot LODGE | 14 | 171 | 0 | | | | | | | | | 2 | 5 | 4 | 3 |
| Christian ELKIN | 13 | 172 | 1 | | | | 13 | | | | | | | | |
| Oliver FITZPATRICK | 13 | 172 | 0 | | | | 5 | | | | 2 | | | | 6 |
| Hafiq AZMI | 11 | 174 | 2 | | 11 | | | | | | | | | | |
| Martin GLOSSOP | 8 | 177 | 3 | | | | | | | 8 | | | | | |
| Simon LOW | 8 | 177 | 0 | 5 | | | 3 | | | | | | | | |
| Alex PERSSON | 7 | 178 | 1 | | | | | | | | | | 7 | | |
| Robert ENGLISH | 7 | 178 | 0 | | | | | 7 | | | | | | | |
| Jon VINCENT | 7 | 178 | 0 | | | | 2 | | 5 | | | | | | |
| Asher DURHAM | 4 | 181 | 3 | | | | | | | | | | | 4 | |
| Sam BURMAN | 3 | 182 | 1 | | | | | | | | 3 | | | | |
| Ricky TARREN | 2 | 183 | 1 | | | | | | | | | | | 2 | |
| Richard FERGUSON | 2 | 183 | 0 | | | | | | 2 | | | | | | |
| Ian STANFORD | 2 | 183 | 0 | | | | 1 | | | | | | 1 | | |
| Max HUNT | 1 | 184 | 1 | | | | | | | | | | | | 1 |
| Jake BAYFORD | 1 | 184 | 0 | | | | | | | | | | | 1 | |
| Joseph THOMAS | 1 | 184 | 0 | | | | | | | | | | 1 | | |
| Greg GREENWOOD | 1 | 184 | 0 | | | | | | | | | 1 | | | |